ENGLISH EXTRA

Key Stage 4

Jeffrey and Lynn Wood

CAMBRIDGE
UNIVERSITY PRESS

Published by the Press Syndicate of the University of Cambridge
The Pitt Building, Trumpington Street, Cambridge CB2 1RP
40 West 20th Street, New York, NY 10011–4211, USA
10 Stamford Road, Oakleigh, Victoria 3166, Australia

© Cambridge University Press 1992

First published 1992

Prepared for publication by Paren & Stacey Editorial Consultants
Designed by Val Grace
Typeset by JCL Data Preparation

Printed in Great Britain by Scotprint Ltd, Musselburgh

A catalogue record for this book is available from the British Library

ISBN 0 521 39872X

Contents

Introduction: To the teacher

Our two **English Extra!** volumes are designed to provide you with a bank of resources.

Their most obvious use is for supply/cover lessons when what is needed (often at short notice) is some structured work which is intrinsically worthwhile, self-contained, complementary to what the class normally does and which calls for the minimum of preparation and administration.

But many of the short stories, poems and creative writing units may slip naturally into your regular teaching programmes – either as extra assignments for particular students who are ahead of/behind the rest of the class or for whole class work. Of course, using them like this may subvert the books' usefulness as cover material. Clearly each department will need a policy on what materials are used and how.

To help departments plan how to use the books, a checklist has been included at the end of each volume which teachers may like to copy in order to keep track of which students have used which materials and when. The checklists summarise the kinds of work each unit covers so that a balanced programme of activities can be planned where a class is using the books over a longer period of time. The checklists also suggest how long each unit is likely to take. Most units lead to a number of activities and we have assumed a) that students will choose which assignments to work on rather than work through them all and b) that a 'session' will be roughly an hour long. Where appropriate, we have made some suggestions for further reading or for further assignments.

We have written with classes of mixed ability in mind. Where there is a substantial text to be read, we hope that whoever is in charge of the lesson will read aloud to the class for a few minutes to get things going.

Experienced English teachers who find themselves 'on cover' at short notice or who are using these materials as part of a regular programme will no doubt intervene at critical points and modify the structure of our units to suit particular students and circumstances. Each lesson is designed to make self-directed work by individuals, by pairs and by small and large groups straightforward, enjoyable and rewarding. Few of the materials we have used figure widely in published school textbooks.

In a very few cases, some forward planning of resources will be necessary – in one of the GCSE units on advertising, for example (see p.87) we ask for the students to have access not just to the random pile of magazines which most English stock rooms possess but to a selection spanning a few years. Such requirements are very much the exception, however, and at the head of these units we show precisely what you will need to provide.

All of the materials are informed by the National Curriculum and GCSE guidelines and there is a careful balance between different kinds of activity – discussion, reading, writing, role-play – so that 'cover' does not become invariably associated either with supervised mayhem or with silent, solo and sullen paper-filling!

Jeffrey & Lynn Wood

Making a poem (i)

THINKING/TALKING POINTS

▶ *In small groups*

'I hope you're listening to what I'm saying!'
'It's lover boy/girl on the phone again.'
'Who's been in the fridge?'
'What does s/he think s/he looks like?'

What are some of the phrases you usually hear at home? Jot down
some of the things people say to you at home which
annoy/embarrass/bore you. Then read this poem.

Don't Interrupt

Turn the television down!
None of your cheek!
Sit down!
Shut up!
Don't make a fool of yourself!
Respect your elders!
I can't put up with you anymore!
Go outside.
Don't walk so fast!
Don't run.
Don't forget to brush your teeth!
Don't forget to polish your shoes!
Don't slam the door!
Have manners!
Don't interrupt when I'm talking!
Put your hand over your mouth when
    you cough.
Don't talk with your mouth full!
Go to the market with me.
You spend too much money!
No more pocket money for you, dear.
Go to your room!
Don't go too near the television.

You're not coming out until you have
    tidied your room.
Don't interrupt when I'm talking!
Did you get any homework today?
Always carry a pen to school.
Eat your dinner up.
Wear your school uniform!
Turn the television over to watch
    'Dallas'.
Bring any letters home from school.
Come straight home tomorrow.
Tidy your bed.
Don't shout!
Don't listen to my conversation.
Don't look at the sun, it could blind
    you.
Don't bite your nails!
Don't suck your thumb!
Why don't you answer me!
You never listen to a word I say!
Don't interrupt when I'm talking!

Demetroulla Vassili

ASSIGNMENT

▶ *On your own or in pairs*

Write your own version of 'Don't Interrupt'. You may like to arrange your
ideas in the same way as Michael Rosen has in his poem 'Parents' Sayings':

P A R E N T S'

SAYINGS

3

2 Talkshop (i)

▷ *In groups of three*

Decide who will be **A**, **B** and **C**. Only **A** and **B** should see the book. Arrange your seats so that **C** is facing the other two but cannot see the pictures.

On the opposite page is a story about a few minutes in somebody's life, told in thirty pictures.

A and **B** take it in turns to tell the story to **C**, one frame at a time.
A and **B** do the story-telling twice - so that **C** gets a really strong idea of what's happening.
Now **C** 'plays back' the story to **A** and **B**, including as much detail as s/he can remember, trying to add nothing new.
A, **B** and **C** look at the pictures together.

◆ What does **C** notice about the similarities/differences between what s/he heard and what s/he sees in the pictures?

◆ Which details did s/he remember most vividly?

Now tell the story again, frame by frame, this time with **C** taking a turn.

Why do you think the story is called 'Eye for an Eye'?

ASSIGNMENT

▷ *On your own or in pairs*

How would the story sound if the person in the pictures were telling it?

What information would be added to what we see in the picture strip?

Either: Tell the story to your partner as a running commentary. Start like this:

'Right! Must make a good impression! Off with the dowdy old glasses, in with the contact lenses! This time I'll make sure they're really clean . . .'

Or: Tell your partner the story of what happened. You could start like this:

'Well, I had plenty of time – or so I thought and you always have to do these things in a relaxed state of mind. I sat down, took off my specs . . .'

eye for an eye

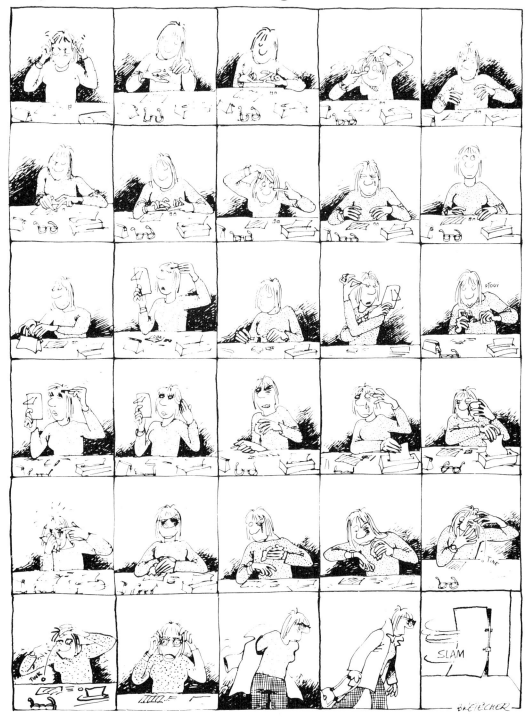

3 Narrative writing (i)

▶

In pairs or small groups

Have you ever been asked to write about 'A Day in the Life of a Pound Coin' or 'Confessions of a Ping-Pong Ball'? Simon Armitage has breathed new life into this old idea. Read through this autobiography of a ten pence piece.

Ten Pence Story

Out of the melting pot, into the mint;
next news I was loose change for a Leeds pimp,
burning a hole in his skin-tight pocket
till he tipped a busker by the precinct.

Not the most ceremonious release
for a fresh faced coin still cutting its teeth.
But that's my point: if you're poorly bartered
you're scuppered before you've even started.

My lowest ebb was a seven month spell
spent head down in a stagnant wishing well,
half eclipsed by an oxidized tuppence
which impressed me with its green circumference.

When they fished me out I made a few phone calls,
fed a few meters, hung round the pool halls.
I slotted in well, but all that vending
blunted my edges and did my head in.

Once, I came within an ace of the end
on the stern of a North Sea ferry, when
some half-cut, ham-fisted cockney tossed me
up into the air and almost dropped me

and every transaction flashed before me
like a time lapse autobiography.
Now, just the thought of travel by water
lifts the serrations around my border.

Some day I know I'll be bagged up and sent
to that knacker's yard for the over spent
to be broken, boiled, unmade and replaced,
for my metals to go their separate ways . . .

which is sad. All coins have dreams. Some castings
from my own batch, I recall, were hatching
an exchange scam on the foreign market
and some inside jobs on one arm bandits.

My own ambition? Well, that was simple:
to be flipped in Wembley's centre circle,
to twist, to turn, to hang like a planet,
to touch down on that emerald carpet.

Those with faith in the system say 'don't quit,
bide your time, if you're worth it, you'll make it.'
But I was robbed, I was badly tendered.
I could have scored. I could have contended.

Simon Armitage

Simon Armitage's poem turns a tired idea into lively writing by working
at key words and phrases. Each stanza describes a stage in the coin's
life. With a head stamped on it and a serrated edge, it is easily damaged,
used in dozens of different ways, in different places by all sorts of
people. But he's writing as if the coin has feelings, hopes and fears.

The best bits of the poem cleverly mix together the hard facts about a
coin with the idea that it's a person:

> *I slotted in well . . .*

Coins feed slot machines. People 'slot in well' when they fit in at work
or in some new situation.

> *. . . inside jobs on one-armed bandits.*

Coins may end up inside one-armed bandits. An 'inside job' is a crime
done by somebody with inside information. The idea of swindling a
bandit (with only one arm) is very neat.

Find some other examples of the poet mixing hard facts about a coin
with the idea that it's human.

ASSIGNMENT

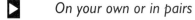 *On your own or in pairs*

See if you can write a piece as lively as Simon Armitage's in which
something tells us about its adventures and its feelings.

Think how you can play with words and phrases so the hard facts about
the object you've chosen can be mixed with human feelings. Find
words which sound like or rhyme with the name of your object.

Here's what one pair of students came up with:

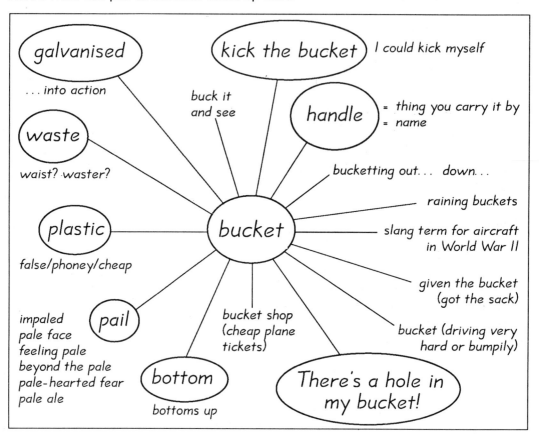

galvanised

. . . into action

kick the bucket   I could kick myself

buck it
and see

handle = thing you carry it by
       = name

waste

waist? waster?

bucketting out. . . down. . .

raining buckets

plastic   bucket   slang term for aircraft
                                         in World War II

false/phoney/cheap

                                         given the bucket
                                         (got the sack)

impaled   pail   bucket shop   bucket (driving very
pale face   (cheap plane   hard or bumpily)
feeling pale   tickets)
beyond the pale
pale-hearted fear   bottom   There's a hole in
pale ale   my bucket!

bottoms up

Either: Experiment with these ideas or ideas of your own to write a
bucket's life story.

Or: Write the autobiography of one of these:

a pair of scissors	a calculator	a telephone
a ball	a rumour	a stamp
a coat-hanger	a joke	a ladder
a knife	a mirror	a credit card
a car tyre	a litre of liquid	a firework
a battery	a can	a raindrop

FOLLOW UP

Have a look at Sylvia Plath's poem 'Mirror'.

4 Poetry workshop (i)

▶ *On your own*

Read this poem.

Love Letter

There must be others in the house,
stuffed in old bags, old shoes, old books especially.
This one turned up in a copy of
'Dr Spock' and *I shall love you always*
stares me in the face along with longings
as bottomless as oceans.
(We were moving over one in a big ship
in separate cabins.)
Consider the ingredients for romance –
one handsome male, unmarried,
one female still in transit, who
could stand as wistfully as any
nineteenth-century heroine at the rail
with mandatory wind in flowing hair,
one baby in her arms (a little out of place here)
then, under the door in the early
hours, this hot and urgent letter . . .
They might have lived together ever after,
but on the envelope my scribbled list of needs reads:
Farex, orange-juice, disposable nappies and
HELP! in capitals. (The child
had had his way with me the whole long
feverish night.)
I'm sure I would have loved you
but the timing wasn't right.

Sylvia Kantaris

Dr Spock – a famous book on child-care

in transit – between one place and the next
wistfully – longingly
mandatory – compulsory

ASSIGNMENT

Either: Write about the voyage as you think the man remembers it. Does he have any mementoes of that trip? What did he feel about the young woman and her child? What are his feelings as he thinks about what might have been?

Or: Write a story about your own romance-which-didn't-happen because 'the timing wasn't right . . .' It could have been:

◆ a school trip – arrangements changed at the last minute

◆ a date – cancelled because of some emergency

◆ a telephone message misunderstood

◆ a sly trick played by a rival

◆ the imagined insult, the mis-overheard remark . . .

5 Descriptive writing (i)

This is a series of related group creative writing exercises which needs somebody to act as Controller.
Materials needed - pens, paper and something firm on which to write.

Sharing An Experience

In Conrad's story, *Heart of Darkness*, Marlow, the story-teller, tries to share with his friends an experience he had many years ago in a far off country. His experiences were terrible and unforgettable. They changed the way Marlow saw everything. As he tries to tell his story, Marlow feels at times that he can never make others understand just what happened to him. How can they see, hear, smell, feel what so disturbed him?

At one point, he breaks down and says:
'No, it is impossible. We live as we dream, alone.'

What do you think he means when he says this?

But Marlow carries on with his story and many readers would say that at least some of those terrible experiences are communicated.

How can we share an experience?

If somebody writes: 'It was so lovely. I felt absolutely at peace. Marvellous. Safe.' All we learn is that X felt like that. We don't **share** the feeling. We're shut out of it, given no information about what made X feel that way.

But if someone writes:

> . . . The cat flattens itself in the gutter,
> Slips out its tongue
> And devours a morsel of rancid butter.

we have a moment's experience, a tingle, a sniff of the atmosphere. And certain feelings come up inside us. The writer's not telling us how to feel, s/he's making us feel it . . . .

WRITER'S WORKSHOP

Stage 1: I am a Microphone

▶ *On your own*

If it's possible, the Controller should open a window and/or a door.

Get absolutely comfortable, close your eyes and listen. After thirty seconds, everyone opens their eyes. Each person in the group describes one thing s/he heard.

11

Now repeat the exercise and listen for much longer – maybe for as long as five minutes. Gradually, the sounds in the room will give way to sounds further and ever further away – in the building and way beyond.

Think about how precisely you can describe each sound you hear. Does the clock tick ? Or would some other words better catch that sound? How did that passing car/train/aeroplane sound different from the last? What tone of voice can you hear next door? What sort of footsteps were those? A horse's? A fat man's? A pygmy's?

What exactly does the wind in the trees sound like – frying fish? somebody sighing? water lapping against pebbles? or what . . .?

Now write down as many of the sounds you heard as you can. Write very quickly at first; then go back over a few details to improve the descriptions, to hunt for exactly the right words. Was it a posh voice? A harsh one? High or low? Was that bump like somebody falling out of bed, two cars colliding, a rap of knuckles on a desk or what . . .?

▶ *In pairs*

Partners can now share what they've collected, compare notes, work together to improve some of the descriptions.

Then each pair tells the rest of the class about one of the sounds they've recorded. People may like to add any descriptions they think are good to their own collection.

Stage 2: Nightmare Scenario

▶ *On your own*

Again get really comfortable and then close your eyes.

You will never see again! The last thing you ever saw was the place you are in now. It contains at least a thousand different things: some big, some small, some valuable, some insignificant. Without peeping, just how many different things in the room can you visualise in your mind's eye?

Just what shade was the carpet? Was there any rubbish on the floor? What was scribbled on the board? In what colour, in what sort of handwriting? What made the chair in which each person is sitting unique? – a wonky leg, a scuff mark, a bit of pink gum stuck on the back? How many of the things pinned around the room can you remember? Were the lights all working? Were the windows dirty or clean? What was on the next desk?

Trying to look only at the paper in front of you, scribble down as many details as you are able to recall.

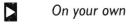 *In pairs*

How many things were you able to remember between you? Again compare notes and work on refining some of your descriptions before reporting one or two of them back to the rest of the class.

Stage 3: Rogues' Gallery

▶ *In groups*

The group sits in a circle, if possible not sitting too closely together, with pens and pads on which to write.

The most important things in the room are the people. At the end of this session, after the class has left, the Controller will be found dead and the police will interview the only member of the class who can be found.

What the police will ask the student to do will be to describe as precisely as possible every other person who was in the room (apart from the body, they have all disappeared without trace).

Write pen-portraits of each person you can see. Take your time. Write not only the police-description-type things – medium build, fair hair, female – but jot down all the details which help to fix each person in your memory: the way s/he moves, speaks, sits; the expression in the eyes, the mouth, her/his gestures. No two people in the room at this moment are sitting in the same way. Concentrate on everything which helps to make each person an individual.

These notes are private. They will not be shared and should be as personal and frank and detailed as possible. Everyone should keep these particular notes concealed.

Stage 4: The Visit

▶ *On your own*

Everyone goes to stand at a window. In two minutes each of you will be asked to write down five different things you have seen, as precisely as possible. Concentrate upon each thing you choose – observe its texture, its precise colour, perhaps the way it is moving. Does that tree resemble an old man or a crane or an octopus or what? How many colours would you need to make a painting of that wall? What's in front of, to the left and right, and behind that crushed Coke can . . .?

▶ *Whole class*

The group returns to base and writes down their descriptions as carefully as they can.

Take it in turns to read out one of them. Again, others in the group may like to 'adopt' any they particularly like.

Stage 5: Being Me

▶ *On your own*

Again close your eyes. This is the last of these sessions. How does that feel?

How exactly does it feel being in your body at this moment? Are your feet warm or cold, sticky, tired or relaxed? What's the feeling behind your eyes? Is the room stuffy or cool? Is your back tense or at ease? Are you feeling peckish? Any aches or pains anywhere? Are your hands clammy or dry? What can you smell? How does your hair feel? What's the taste in your mouth? Any jagged teeth, raw fingernails, clothes which don't quite fit?

Concentrate on physical feelings: if you feel relaxed, how does that register itself in your body? If you're tired, what exactly does that **feel** like? Heavy limbs? Breathing laboured? Jaw sagging?

After five minutes or so, write up what you registered in your body.

ASSIGNMENT

Under the title 'Here and Now' write the time and date of this workshop.

Using as much of all the data you have collected in the five exercises as you can, see if you can write a description of what it was like being in this particular session, in this particular place, on this particular day: a record of what it was like being you for that hour. Make it a description so full of vivid details that in twenty years' time you will be able to read it and relive this hour's experience.

6 Making a poem (ii)

▶ *In pairs or small groups*

Dictionaries and thesauruses, and a highlighter pen would be handy.

WRITER'S WORKSHOP

One way of making a poem is to **brainstorm**. This means working with a partner or a group to come up with as many words, phrases, ideas as you can about the subject you have chosen.

If you can use a tape recorder, you can collect your ideas as they pop up. Otherwise someone needs to jot things down as quickly as possible.

Stage 1

Close your eyes. What do you see, hear, feel when somebody says the word **cat**?

Here are some things one group of students came up with:

> *dustbin raiders   smelly   clean as a cat's yawn   pouncing*
> *Tom and Jerry   like feather dusters   sharp ears   smugfaced   lazy*
> *restless, always on the go   boiled fish at my old piano teacher's house*
> *alleycats   fangs and claws that catch   chasing a ball of wool*
> *needlesharp   sly   witches' cats   scream like kids being tortured*
> *dirty old tomcat   curly tails   tails sticking up straight*
> *tails like rope   like snakes   muck in our garden   silent and strong*
> *snooty   aristocratic   aristocats   not very friendly   independent*
> *proud   stand-offish   affectionate   untrustworthy*
> *you can't get round one like you can a dog   cuddly   cosy*
> *cruel, playing with their victims   sleek-head   stretching*
> *arching its back   sinister   beautiful bright green eyes   hypnotic*
> *black cat for luck   nightprowlers   catflaps   Whiskas   miaow*
> *caterwauling   milk in a saucer   kittens in a basket*

Stage 2

When you have found as many words and phrases as you can by brainstorming like this, you may like to use a **thesaurus** to see what else you can come up with.

If you look up **cat** in a thesaurus, you find these words:

> *feline   gib   grimalkin   malkin   mawkin   mog   moggy*
> *mouser   puss   pussy   tabby*

Pick **feline** and look up that in the thesaurus and you get more words:

> *catlike   graceful   leonine   seductive   sensual   sinuous   sleek*
> *slinky   smooth   stealthy*

Picking out the word **slinky** leads to:

clinging   close-fitting   figure-hugging   lean   skin-tight

And if then you follow up **graceful**, you find:

*agile balletic beautiful becoming charming comely deft
easy elegant facile feat fine flowing fluid gainly
gracile lightsome natural pleasing pliant slender
smooth suave supple tasteful willowish willowy . . .*

It's not unusual for a brainstorming session followed by a thesaurus
hunt to give you a heap of more than a hundred words and phrases.
Let's see what we've got so far:

*dustbin raiders   smelly   clean as a cat's yawn   pouncing
Tom and Jerry   like feather dusters   sharp ears   smugfaced   lazy
restless, always on the go   boiled fish at my old piano teacher's house
alleycats   fangs and claws that catch   chasing a ball of wool
needlesharp   witches' cats   scream like kids being tortured
sly   dirty old tomcat   curly tails   tails sticking up straight
tails like rope   like snakes   muck in our garden   silent and strong
snooty   aristocratic   aristocats   not very friendly   stretching
independent   proud   stand-offish   affectionate   untrustworthy
you can't get round one like you can a dog   cuddly   cosy
cruel, playing with their victims   sleek-head   arching its back
sinister   beautiful bright green eyes   hypnotic   black cat for luck
nightprowlers   catflaps   Whiskas   miaow   caterwauling
milk in a saucer   kittens in a basket   feline   gib   grimalkin
malkin   mawkin   mog   moggy   mouser   puss   pussy   tabby
catlike   graceful   leonine   seductive   sensual   sinuous   sleek
slinky   smooth   stealthy   clinging   close-fitting   figure-hugging
lean   skin-tight   agile   balletic   beautiful   becoming
charming   comely   deft   easy   elegant   facile   feat   fine
flowing   fluid   gainly   gracile   lightsome   natural   pleasing
pliant   slender   smooth   suave   supple   tasteful   willowish
willowy*

Stage 3

Now close your eyes. Think of, try to picture clearly in your mind's eye,
a particular cat in a particular place, for example:

◆ your own cat first thing in the morning or when you play with it in
  the garden

◆ a neighbour's cat

◆ a cat chasing pigeons

◆ a cat on the roof . . .

Look at the heap of words you've got about cats. Use a highlighter pen to pick out all the words and phrases which would fit in a piece of writing about that particular cat. These are some you might choose for a poem called 'Dustbin Raider'.

> *pouncing   sharp ears   restless, always on the go   alleycats   sly*
> *tails like rope   independent   nightprowlers   caterwauling*
> *stealthy*

As the movements of the cat, its character begin to take shape in your imagination, think a bit about the setting, the time of day. Develop some ideas around each detail, for example:

◆ night time. . .   crimetime   black as soot   city lights   shadows
  silence   wail of a siren   trees creaking

◆ alleyway. . .   litter   broken glass   bottles and cans   footsteps
  creepy

◆ dustbins. . .   clatter   fishbones   smelly   neglected
  some fallen over

Gradually see how you might begin to shape these different ideas, to put them together to make a collage of words to make a cat poem or a story. Here's what one student wrote:

Dark Tom

Dustbin raider prowling the alleyways,
Picks his way daintily over broken glass,
Brushes a coke can
Sharp ears pricked . . .
Sudden footsteps behind
A clatter, a scream . . .

ASSIGNMENT

Either: Use the materials here to write a piece of your own about a particular cat. Here are some titles you might use:

Wildcat; Sophisticat; Shadow, the Midnight Cat . . .

Begin by turning back to the list of words on page 16. Select all the words which match your particular cat. Then work through the stages which follow until you have your own cat poem.

Or: Use the techniques described in this unit to write a piece about one of the following:

a hawk   Christmas   the storm   two tramps   Spring   a party

7 | Short story workshop (i)

THINKING/TALKING POINTS

▶ *In groups*

◆ What do you understand by the word ghost?

◆ What ghost stories do you know?

◆ What things do you think make the difference between a terrifying ghost story and a silly one?

Imagine your group has been asked to write a ghost story for a competition. What setting(s) would you choose? (What kind of building? Time of year? Weather? Landscape?) Discuss some descriptive details you might use.

What sort of characters do you think would be most likely to be 'haunted'? (A dreamer? Someone who had a guilty conscience? Someone who had lost a close friend/ relative? Someone whose life was happy and uncomplicated . . .?)

How would you present your 'ghost' so it was more disturbing than ridiculous?

What ghost story formulas and clichés would you try to avoid?

Here's a ghost story by Joan Aiken. You may like to listen while somebody reads it aloud, read it silently to yourselves or read it around the group, taking a sentence each in turn.

Power Cut

The wind, like a flapping blanket, beat and thrashed and swung and slapped and buffeted, making each casement rattle, every door sway and creak. The wind sighed in the chimney, clanked in the pipes, and gibbered in the TV aerial. Rain slammed on to the slates, and dashed in cascades against the stuttering windows. The cottage was massively built, its two-foot thick rock walls were solidly planted on a Cornish hillside. It bore with indifference the lash of the gale. But all the air inside was disturbed, full of pockets and sudden eddies; in spite of closed doors and shuttered windows, the weather seemed to pass right through the house as if, Thomas felt, it were only a skeleton house, a diagram of a building. He put out his hand to feel the wall. It felt thick, immovable, though chill and sweating with damp; but as soon as he removed his hand, the fluttering air suggested to him again that he was standing in the middle of the moor.

Or in the middle of nowhere.

He called, 'Celia? Where are you?'

Her voice came from above. 'I'm upstairs. Switching on all the heaters. Airing the blankets. Everything feels horribly damp. Why

casement – window frame

gibbered – sounded like a mad babbling

with indifference – not worried

eddies – little whirlpools

blasted old Mrs Tredinnick couldn't come as I asked her to and switch on the nightstores . . . Can you turn on the fan heater in the living room?'

'Okay.'

He felt his way along the side of the kitchen, navigating by the feel of the smooth, square metal shapes. Refrigerator, cooking-stove, clothes-washer, dryer, dish-washer, two steel sinks (with rubbish disposal unit in one), electric furnace, then a cupboard. Then came the door into the living room. From twenty years of living in it, he knew their London house intimately, so that he had no need to feel his way, could walk freely from room to room. But the cottage was strange territory nowadays; he had not set foot in it for seven or eight years. Had not wanted to.

It had been a happy retreat when they first bought it – bare and primitive though it had been. It was surrounded by grass and heather, a place to come for weekends and holidays with the children, where they half-camped, cooking sausages on sticks over peat fires. Those times were far in the past. They had swum in the old quarry, which the children nick-named The Bottomless Pool (the children wearing life-jackets at all times in case of cramp from the nerve-chilling cold of the water); they had fished in the stream and taken immense walks on the moor.

Then, later, the cottage had become a refuge. They had come on escape-weekends, fleeing from those same children, grown large now, and defiant, inhabiting the London house with their friends like advance occupying forces from a hostile planet. During that period they had taken pains (or Celia had – he had little interest in the process) to render the cottage more comfortable, putting in electricity with all its benefits: radio, TV, a deep-freeze so there was always food in store, more furniture, carpets and colour-schemes. Celia's friend the interior decorator Gerard Barron had contributed the colour schemes. And the result of that was an article, with pictures, in one of the colour-supplements.

Then there had been a period when Celia came for weekends on her own, or with Gerard Barron.

Then there had been the period when, theoretically, the cottage had been ceded to their eldest son, Simon. In theory Simon had paid rent for it. That period had lasted for an uneasy three or four years, punctuated with battles:

'When did that boy last pay you any rent? Come on now – has he paid any at all this year?'

'Well –'

'Well what?'

'He did give me two of his pictures. In a gallery they'd fetch a hundred pounds at least –'

'A gallery? Hah! What gallery? Booker looked at some of them

nightstores – electric heaters which come on at night

navigating – finding his way

retreat – place to escape to

peat – turf used like coal

refuge – place of safety

defiant – refusing to do as they were told

render – make

ceded – given

punctuated with – interrupted by

and told me they looked as if they'd been done by a demented four-year-old. That rent has got to be paid in *cash* – or he has to clear out – he and those friends of his! God knows what goes on in that place.'

demented – crazy

Then Celia, returning from a weekend in Looe (with whom, he had not inquired; not with Gerard Barron, that was long finished) had called at the cottage and found nobody there. 'But the *mess*, Thomas! I was really appalled! All our beautiful colour-schemes covered over with crazy murals. Mud and cigarette ends all over the carpets. They're absolutely ruined. Dirt everywhere. The windows painted silver so you can't see out. The furniture half scraped – that valuable rosewood table! I could have burst out crying. I've *never* been so upset in my whole *life*.'

murals – wall paintings

Simon had been equally angry.

'But you *gave* me the cottage! You said it was mine, that I could do what I liked with it.'

'Not to wreck our expensive furniture. Not to turn the whole place into a disgusting shambles. Eating off the floor! Leaving the dish-washer open to rust – smashing the TV screen!'

'That's the way I and my friends *like* to live – we can do without all your ridiculous pampering luxury, your endless gadgets. Even an answering device on the phone – in the middle of Bodmin Moor, for Christ's sake!'

After that, Simon had been told to get out of the cottage, and after some more dispute, he had left, saying to his mother that he would never forgive her; for tax reasons, the cottage was said to belong to Celia.

for tax reasons – to save on income tax

She had had the place redecorated and tidied up, but this time her heart was not in it.

After that, for a period of several years, it had been used less and less.

And then, and then . . .

He had switched on the fan heater in the living-room, which smelt depressingly of mildew, and then returned to the kitchen. Here the chimney was blocked; the howl of the gale was less audible.

audible – easily heard

'Anything you'd like me to do?' he called up the stairs.

'No . . . no,' Celia's voice came down impatiently. 'Well – yes; switch on the electric cooker – that'll help dry the place out.'

He felt his way to the cooker and located the switch. After a moment, holding his hands a few inches above the top of the stove, he could feel the plates begin to glow.

located – found

They were here to try and mend their marriage; a hopeless project, perhaps. The weather certainly wasn't helping; terrible for early June. They were here to try to recover from Simon's death. And their own feelings towards each other about it. They were here to tidy and clear out the cottage so that it could be sold. They were here to bury Simon's memory.

'I won't have that boy in the house another *day*. I tell you.'

'But Thomas – he's been so ill. He looks so terrible. If you could only see him –'

That had been a tactical error on Celia's part.

'I don't need to see him, thank you. I can smell him – where he's been smoking that stuff. *And* hear him. If he puts that bloody record on once more – "Gimme, gimme, gimme all you pro-o-o-mised me!" '

Then the police had come round. A pound of cannabis had been found in Simon's room.

'No I am *not* going to pay his bail. Let him stew in his own juice. I wash my hands of him. If you hadn't spoiled him rotten – given him all he ever asked for –'

'Oh, you're just a cold-hearted, vindictive bastard – I truly believe you still hold it against him – after all these years – over twenty years now –'

Twenty years of not being able to see. Did she think that the length of time reduced the sense of loss? Twenty years since he had been able to look at the black-and-blue stormy sky which he had to imagine careering past overhead; the patches of steel-and-amber coloured light and the rain-squalls chasing each other over the moor.

'For heaven's sake, he was only a tiny boy then, four years old – He didn't know what he was doing –'

A spoilt, strong, tyrannical four-year-old with a grievance and a can of aerosol oven-spray.

There came a loud, sharp knock at the back door. Even above the wail and gibber of the wind he could hear its peremptory summons – bang-bang – and a pause – bang-bang again.

'Celia!' he called. 'There's someone at the back door.'

'Well answer it, then! Don't be so bloody helpless,' she called impatiently. 'I'm in the middle of making up the beds.'

He felt his way out of the kitchen, along the narrow slate-floored back passage, where the original granite of the cottage could still be felt. And smelt. He fumbled past coats hanging on hooks. The back door was still locked. He turned the key, pressing with both hands to move it in its rusty socket, and opened the door. A gust of rain slapped him in the face, as if the weather were seizing this chance to take more tangible possession of the cottage.

'Yes?' he said. 'Hullo – who is it?' He had caught Celia's impatience. 'Who is there?'

He recognised the cracked old voice, though he had not heard it recently.

'It's Anna Tredinnick, Mr Michaels. I came to ask about my cat.'

'Oh, good evening, Mrs Tredinnick. Why –'

Why the hell didn't you turn on the nightstores, as my wife wrote and asked you to, he felt like saying, but then thought better. No sense in antagonising the old girl, who was their nearest neighbour, the only caretaker they had been able to secure. He amended his question to,

'Why don't you come in?'

'No', she said. 'I won't do that. I'm all wet. – I'm all wet', she repeated, in her singsong, west-country voice. 'Just feel how wet I am, Mr Michaels.' And she took his hand before he could prevent her, and guided it over what felt like the stiff wrinkles of some sodden, felted-up material. He removed his hand with fastidious speed as soon as he could withdraw it from her cold, skinny old claw.

'Well –' he said irritably. What was that about her cat?

'Your cat, Mrs Tredinnick? What about your cat?'

'The young 'un. Simon. When he was here. He had the old puss up to the cottage. He were always mortal fond o' cats, young Simon.'

'*Simon* had it here? But we told you, Mrs Tredinnick, that you were on *no* account to let him have the key – on no account to let him *into* the cottage. We told you he wasn't to be allowed to use it any more, after what he and his friends did before.' (Besides – *when* was he at the cottage?)

'Ah, I told him that, Mr Michaels. "You bean't allowed to go in there no more", I told him. "You better go off somewhere else, afore I call the police, like Mr Michaels says I got to." "You mind your blurry business, you old hag", he says to me. Proper rude, he was. He didn't take no notice o' me. He had his own key, see? *I* couldn't stop him. And the pussy was up here, too. The old puss always did go up, if ever young Simon was there. So then I did call the police, and Sergeant Pollard from Bodmin, he come out – and I give him my key to the place – but young Simon he were gone by then. Likely he just come to fetch summat he left behind. But since then the old puss he haven't been back home; no, I haven't seen him since that day.'

'Well I'm very sorry, Mrs Tredinnick, but there's no cat here. You're welcome to come in and look around if you want –'

Just the same, he very much hoped that the old thing wouldn't, she smelt perfectly disgusting, of wet, muddy, dirty wool and damp, unwashed old age.

'If your cat had been shut in here, it would surely have run out as soon as we opened up the house –'

No, though; it might not have, he thought, gagging a little, on the stench of wet old woman, and the thought that just then occurred to him.

'Ah – how long ago *was* this, Mrs Tredinnick? When was my son here?'

For it was not five weeks since Simon, released from his eighteen-month term, had been found burned to death in somebody's barn

antagonising – making her an enemy
amended – changed

fastidious – not liking to touch her

mortal – very

bean't – aren't

summat – something

gagging – feeling sick

term – jail sentence

22

together with the barn itself, and most of the hay it contained. Careless smoking, was the verdict. Death by misadventure. Simon must have come to the cottage shortly before? To collect some cache he had left here? Or hoping to stay, after being turned ruthlessly away from the London house?

cache – something hidden

'No, Simon. This isn't your home any more. I'm sorry.'

He had not been sorry. He had been immensely relieved.

But if the cat had been shut in the cottage five weeks, it could not have survived.

'Celia?' he called nervously up the stairs. 'Mrs Tredinnick's here, asking about her cat. You – you haven't seen a cat anywhere?'

'What? I can't hear you.'

He walked to the foot of the stairs and repeated his question. After a moment or two Celia came running down.

'For God's sake, shut that back door!' she snapped. 'Half the Atlantic's blowing into the house – there's a lake in the back passage already!'

Impatiently she pushed past him and slammed the rattling door.

'But Mrs Tredinnick's out there!'

'No she isn't. There was nobody outside.'

'Are you sure?'

'Positive.'

'Oh well,' he said. 'I suppose the old girl must have gone off again as soon as she was certain the cat wasn't here. I suppose you *haven't* seen a cat anywhere? She sounded a bit distraught about it. I hope it's not shut in somewhere.' He sniffed. 'I can't stand the smell.'

distraught – very upset

'Thomas.' Celia's voice, too, sounded strange, he noticed.

'Yes, what?'

'Simon must have been here. Before – before. His bed had been slept in. He must have spent a night here.'

'Yes', he said. 'The old girl just said so. Simon must have had a key we didn't know about. But she called the police, and by the time they turned up, he had left.'

'Oh god, oh *god*!' From the sound, he could tell that Celia must have sat by the kitchen table and laid her head on her arms. 'Poor wretched boy – hounded about – from place to place – as if he were some kind of *monster* – ending up in that barn –'

'He *was* some kind of monster,' Thomas said coldly. 'He had completely abandoned the rules of civilised behaviour.'

'How could you just *abandon* your own *child*?'

'Shut up, Celia!' We've been through all this – over and over. There's no sense in having it all again. Get a grip on yourself, for god's sake. Here we are, out in the middle of the moor, in the middle of a bloody tempest – this just isn't the time for hysterics.'

tempest – storm

'I can't think why we came here', she said abruptly. The chair scraped; her voice shifted; she had stood up. 'It's hopeless. This place is haunted. It was crazy to come –'

'We had to come some time', he pointed out reasonably. 'If we're going to sell the place, we've got to tidy it, and find out what's here. Come on – pull yourself together. You'll solve no problems by running away.'

'Running away? Isn't that what you've been doing all *along*?' she said furiously. 'Running away from the problems of your own – *Oh!*'

'What's up *now*?' he said, for her last exclamation seemed to have no connection with the preceding words.

'All the lights have gone out. Power failure I suppose. The gale must have blown down a cable somewhere. That's *really* torn it. We can't stay in this place if nothing's working.'

'Why? it probably won't last long. We can burn candles. I expect there's still some peat in the shed.'

'Don't be stupid! We'd freeze! Everything's sopping. Besides, we can't cook, or heat the water – or even *get* any water if the electric pump's not working –'

A drawer rattled; she appeared to be hunting for candles. She said, and he could hear panic in her voice. 'My god, it's so *dark*! I'd forgotten how pitch dark it is out here on the moor.'

Now you know how dark it is where I am, he thought.

'There don't seem to be any candles. Simon must have used them all.'

Took them to set fire to the hay in that barn? he wondered.

'I'll phone Mrs Tredinnick and see if she has any.'

But the phone in the living-room was dead, too, when he tried it; presumably the gale had cut out the telephone, as well as the power lines. Replacing the receiver, he knocked his elbow, as he rememberd doing so many times in the past, on the shelf that held the recorded-message gadget. Swearing absently, he rubbed his arm. In doing so he must accidentally have switched on the machine, for his own voice suddenly spoke out, loud and harsh, just above his right ear.

absently – without realising

'Simon: listen. Simon. This is just to tell you that, if by any chance, you should turn up at the cottage, Mrs Tredinnick has our instructions to call the police. You are not – repeat, *not* – to use the cottage. Is that understood?'

Amplified to twice its volume, his voice sounded harsh, but also nervous; there seemed to be a note of crazy pleading in its threat.

By contrast, the voice of his son was merely mocking.

'Hello, Dad, dear Daddy? By the time you get this, I'll be gone-o – so you'll be able to enjoy the pleasures of the place all on your own. All on your loney-own, won't that be nice for you, Daddy? You can use the polisher, the blender, the vacuum-cleaner, the dish-washer, the garbage-destructor – you'd better use *that*, daddy, that'll be just what you need – you can watch the telly, you can listen to the radio, even, as a special treat, you can listen to some of my discs. *Won't that be fun?* You can cook yourself some scrumptious frozen *lasagne*, and cuddle up in bed with your electric blanket. But, before you have supper, if I were you, I'd look in the dish-washer, Daddy, because old Mrs Busy Tredinnick may be wanting her cat, and it might have got in there. You know how cats are, Daddy. Right? Right. So long then. Love from Simon.'

The tape ran to its end and began to squeal. Then it cut out.

I can't really have heard that, he thought, after a moment. I must have imagined it.

It can't have been switched on, because the power is off.

Is it off, still?

He tried the telephone. It was still dead. Feeling his way back to the kitchen, he called,

'Celia, hey Celia?'

'What?' her voice came from the coat-rack near the back door. It was muffled, as if she were putting on a hood.

'Is the power still off?'

'Yes, it is. I'm going down to Mrs Tredinnick to borrow some candles.'

'Walking?'

'In this weather? Are you kidding? No, I'm taking the car. If she hasn't any I'll knock up the shop.'

'You'll come back?' He despised the pleading in his own voice.

'Yes.' But did she mean it? He was not sure.

The front door slammed. Instantly after its bang he heard another noise: the howl of a cat, the loud, resonant, desperate wauling cry of a cat that has been shut up in a box or basket and is frantic to get out. The whole house seemed to reverberate with its miaowing.

reverberate – echo

Thomas hated cats – couldn't stand them anywhere near him, or in the house at all. Early on, *that* had had to be made plain to the children, who had, at times, begged for kittens, offered by ignorant neighbours. Once, Simon had actually brought one home; it had had to be taken back to its place of origin.

Thomas went to the front door and opened it, shouting, 'Celia, Celia! Just a minute. That bloody old woman's cat *is* in here somewhere. Come back!'

But the sound of the car's engine was his only answer, just audible above the roar of the wind.

He went back to the kitchen. And now the cat's frenzied yelling seemd to be coming from one distinct point. Groping his way past refrigerator, cooker (now gone stone-cold again), Laundrymaster, spin-dryer, he came to the dish-washer, which seemed to be vibrating from the urgency to be free of the creature trapped inside it. Lucky nobody switched it on, Thomas thought.

But why had the cat not cried before? And how could it have survived five weeks, shut in there?

No need to ask *who* shut it in, he thought, pulling down the hinged front panel.

He expected a furry body to shoot out past him and escape. But that was not what happened. The howling went on. Was the cat somehow tied in there, trapped?

Gingerly, with acute repugnance, Thomas extended a cautious hand in among the framework of racks which made up the interior of the machine – and then pulled back his hand with a cry of disgust and fright even louder than the yells of the trapped creature itself. He had touched a mess of cold, congealed slimy fur and bone, which gave, horribly, under his exploring fingers.

Cursing, he jumped towards the sink and turned the tap, wishing to wash the revolting scummy slime off his fingers. But no water came from the tap. He had to grope in a drawer for a towel and rub, rub, rub at his hands. Nothing would shift the memory of that horrible contact.

Now the whole kitchen seemed filled with the stink of wet fur and cat's urine. And now he knew what that crazy, wicked, revengeful boy meant when he said, 'You better use the garbage destructor, Daddy – that'll be just what you need.'

How could Simon *do* such a thing? A boy who had loved cats?

In the blacked-out village Celia was knocking in vain at the door of Mrs Tredinnick's cottage. A neighbour, passing with a torch, told her, 'You'll find nobody to home, therr, midear. Hadn't you heard, then? The old lady was drowned in the pool, top o' moor, last Friday week, that black foggy night. 'Tis thought she were out a-hunting for her puss . . .'

And in the pitch-dark cottage kitchen Thomas, standing rigid with horror, heard the voice of the wind begin to abate. But, taking its place, the sounds of man-made power inside the cottage began to rise and menace: the refrigerator hummed and stuttered, the spin-dryer roared, the vacuum-cleaner surged, the telephone maniacally rang, the television boomed, the blender chattered, the garbage-destructor rumbled, and a disc on the record-player, turned up to a shattering intensity of sound yelled,

'*Gimme*, GIMME, *GIMME* all you *PROMISED* meee . . .'

Thomas opened the front door and ran out, taking his own darkness with him.

gingerly – very carefully
with acute repugnance – hating what he had to do
congealed – liquid which has almost gone solid

abate – die away

26

THINKING/TALKING POINTS

▶ *On your own or in pairs*

See how many of the details of Simon's life and death you are able to reconstruct. What was his relationship with his parents like? Why?

Pick out half a dozen details which you think help to make this ghost story a) believable and b) disturbing.

Which supernatural details do you find most/least effective? Explain why.

Before you work on one of the assignments, read through 'Power Cut' again. See how many details Joan Aiken has put into her story which mean more on second reading.

ASSIGNMENT

▶ *On your own or in pairs*

Either: Write an essay about Joan Aiken's story 'Power Cut'. Do you think it is an exciting ghost story? Discuss three or four moments from the story in some detail, saying what you liked/disliked about the way those parts of the story were written.

Or: Write a ghost story of your own in which some injury, mistake done in the past comes back to haunt someone.

Or: See if you can write a couple of pages of a story called 'Kidnapped'. It is told by somebody who has been blindfolded, taken somewhere and left.

In 'Power Cut', Thomas, Simon's father, relies on his senses of touch, smell and hearing to work out where he is and what is happening.

Your piece might begin like this:

'It was getting chillier now and the voices faded into the distance . . .

What can you tell about your surroundings? Are you inside/outside? Is it day/night? What's the weather? Any clues as to where you are? In the country? in town? in a cellar or in an attic?

What can you hear/smell/touch as you explore your 'prison'?

What are your feelings?, hopes, fears? How can you escape?

Remember to keep some things unexplained and mysterious.

8 | Working from pictures (i)

▶

FOR DISCUSSION

In pairs

A dictionary and/or thesaurus would be handy.

Study the picture opposite for a few minutes before considering the questions below.

Suggest some titles for this picture.

Why do you think the photographer chose to shoot this picture in black and white? How do you think colour would alter the impact of the picture?

In what sort of place(s) do you think this shot might have been taken?

If we could hear, smell, touch as well as see this place, what words would you choose from this list to describe it?

> cold   clammy   eerie   warm   silent   subterranean   oily
> thundering   wet   dry   lonely   noisy   harsh   sterile   dreamy
> cosy   claustrophobic   grubby   moving   friendly   oppressive

Add some words of your own to any you have chosen.

What do you think the man feels about what he's doing?

Look carefully at the way the man is standing. Find some words and phrases to describe it.

ASSIGNMENT

Either: See if you can translate this picture into a 'picture in words'.

Don't just include 'information', for example, 'a man wearing a grubby vest, holding a huge spanner . . .' See if you can convey the particular mood the photographer has captured, for example, 'the man seems to be in a prison of pipes and brutal machinery . . .'

Or: Imagine yourself doing the man's job. Write his thoughts and feelings about his work.

♦   What is his attitude to the machinery?

♦   What does he feel his job doing to him as a person?

♦   What chances has he of getting out of that situation?

♦   How does he feel about the owners of the factory?

You might begin like this:

> 'Another five hours to go. Still only Wednesday. How much longer?'

9 Working from pictures (ii)

▶

On your own or in pairs
Look carefully at the picture opposite for a few moments.

THINKING/TALKING POINTS

◆ Where do you think this scene takes place? Suggest a time of day. A season of the year.

◆ How many people are involved? What seems to be their attitude
   a) to what they're doing?
   b) to each other?

◆ Describe carefully what was happening at the moment when the photograph was taken. What sounds do you imagine in the place?

◆ What words would you choose to describe the mood here?

   tranquil   hectic   tense   sleepy   sombre . . .?

◆ If you were painting a picture of this scene, what would you concentrate upon?

◆ Now try to imagine this place an hour before the photograph was taken.
   What details would be the same as they are in the picture?
   What would be different?

◆ How do you imagine the scene as it might have been an hour after the photograph was taken?

◆ Suggest a title for the picture.

ASSIGNMENTS

Imagine you are one of the people in the picture.
Describe what is going on as if s/he were speaking.
Concentrate not only on what can be seen, but on sounds, smells and atmosphere, too.
What is s/he feeling about the people around him/her?
How does s/he feel about what's happening?
Give your piece a title.

Write a story about the person whose place is empty.

10 Poetry workshop (ii)

▶ *On your own*

See if you can remember a time in your life when you were the centre of attention, for example:

◆ in a fight in the playground

◆ the morning your name was mentioned in assembly

◆ the moment when you blew out the candles on a birthday cake

◆ performing in front of an audience

◆ climbing a tree whilst everyone watched . . .

Close your eyes for a moment and see exactly what you can remember:

◆ What were you wearing? What sort of day was it?

◆ Where exactly were you? What did the place look like?

◆ See if you can remember people's remarks, expressions as they watched you.

◆ How did you feel? scared? proud? embarrassed? sticky? cool?

◆ What else can remember about that moment? what smells, what colours? what noises?

▶ *In pairs*

Decide who will be **A** and who will be **B**.
A describes to **B** a moment when s/he was the centre of attention.
Now **B** 'plays back' what **A** said, including as many details as s/he can remember.
Now **B** describes to **A** a moment when everyone's attention was on him/her.
A retells **B**'s story, including as much detail as possible.

▶ *Whole class*

Here is a poem by Theodore Roethke about a childhood moment he recalls vividly. We don't know why he was on top of the greenhouse or what people thought of it; what he gives us is a snapshot from his past:

Child on Top of a Greenhouse

The wind billowing out the seat of my britches
My feet crackling splinters of grass and dried putty,
The half-grown chrysanthemums staring up like accusers,
Up through the streaked glass, flashing with sunlight,
A few white clouds all rushing eastward,
A line of elms plunging and tossing like horses,
And everyone, everyone pointing up and shouting!

Theodore Roethke

FOR DISCUSSION

How many different pieces of information are we given in those seven lines?

Which details give you a strong sense of what it felt like standing up there? What does each detail make you imagine? How does it make you feel?

See how many different explanations you can think of for the boy climbing up on top of the greenhouse.

How do you imagine the faces of the people watching him? What might they be shouting?

ROLE-PLAY

 In pairs

Read through 'Child on Top of a Greenhouse' again and then try out this exercise.

One of you is the owner of the greenhouse, the other is the boy.

Improvise the conversations they might have when the boy finally comes down. Try out the conversation a few times, swapping roles.

Each time give the two characters different sorts of personality. Try out lots of different explanations and reactions. It's up to you which of them (if either) is honest with the other.

Here are some characters you may like to explore:

♦ a naughty boy who climbed up to do some damage

♦ a brave boy who was trying to rescue a cat

♦ a timid boy who was trying to impress his mates

♦ a frightened boy who was running away from something

♦ an owner who blames the boy for all the damage that's been done to his property recently

♦ an owner who was frightened the boy would hurt himself on his dangerous building

♦ an owner who used to do the same sort of thing himself when he was a boy.

ASSIGNMENT

▶ *On your own*

Write about a moment when everyone's attention was on you. See if you can include lots of information so that the reader can imagine what it felt like being you. Write in verse or prose.

Descriptive writing (ii)

▶   *In pairs or whole class*

Here are some descriptions of faces.

Read through each one (or better still, listen to somebody else reading it to you). Close your eyes and see what kind of mental picture you form of the person being described.

Faces That You Meet

Hernan was a very big man with a square muscular head. His face was tanned brown by the elements. He was all fairhaired and his face had the gentle, passive expression of the man who never thinks of anything but physical things. An ever-active, fearless man.

(from *Trapped* by Liam O'Flaherty)

My cabbie was fortyish, lean, balding. Such hair as remained scurried long and damp down his neck and shoulders . . . This mad neck was explosively pocked and mottled, with a flicker of adolescent virulence in the crimson underhang of the ears . . . His face was much nastier, tastier, altogether more useful than I had banked on it being — barnacled and girlish with bright eyes and prissy lips, as if there were another face, the real face, beneath his mask of skin.

(from *Money* by Martin Amis)

The prisoner was waiting to be fed, looking sideways through the bars . . . with much of the expression of a wild beast . . . But his eyes, too close together, were not so nobly set in his head as those of the king of beasts are in his, and they were sharp rather than bright — pointed weapons with little surface . . . They had no depth or change; they glittered and they opened and shut . . . a clockmaker could have made a better pair.

He had a hook nose, handsome after its kind but too high between the eyes by probably as much as his eyes were too near to one another . . .

When Monsieur Rigaud laughed, a change took place in his face . . . His moustache went up under his nose, and his nose came down over his moustache, in a very sinister and cruel manner.

(from *Little Dorrit* by Charles Dickens)

. . . a thin lad with a bony face that was always pale, except for two rosy spots on his cheekbones. He had quick brown eyes, short wiry hair.

(from *Spit Nolan* by Bill Naughton)

He was laughing, chin up, and shaking his head. God the father was exploding in his face with a glory of sunlight through painted glass, a glory that moved with his movements to consume and exalt Abraham and Issac and the God again. The tears of laughter in his eyes made additional spokes and wheels and rainbows. Chin up . . . eyes half closed; joy . . .

(from *The Spire* by William Golding)

THINKING/TALKING POINTS

Without re-reading the passages, see how many of these questions you can answer:

◆ One of the characters was a prisoner. What were his eyes like? Describe his expression when he laughed.

◆ What colour was Hernan's face? Why was it that colour?

◆ Which of the characters might have been a priest? How do you know?

◆ What was distinctive about the thin lad's cheeks?

◆ What can you remember about the cab driver's face?

ASSIGNMENT

▶ *On your own or in pairs*

It is only by studying a face for a long time that it is possible to produce pen-portraits like these. It's usually impossible to do this unless it's in a life-drawing class.

Here are some photographs to study. Pick one which interests you and then try the following:

1 Study the photograph for a few minutes, making a mental note of the distinctive features as if you were going to draw them.

2 Turn the photograph away and see how vividly you can see it in your mind's eye. Which feature(s) do you recall? What mood did the face suggest? What sort of person? Jot down some words and phrases to recapture the face.

3 Look at the picture again to see how sharp your recollection was. Had you forgotten anything important?

4 Now see if you can turn the photograph into a pen-portrait similar to the ones which you read at the beginning of this unit.

5 When you are pleased with what you have written, you may like to swap your completed version with somebody else in the class. See if you can tell which picture each of you is describing.

12 Poetry workshop (iii)

THINKING/TALKING POINTS

▶ *In pairs or small groups*

Can you recall asking a grown-up about things which puzzled you and being fobbed off with half an answer or no answer at all? What questions do you remember adults refusing to answer?

Do you think that there are things that parents should not tell children? At what age do you think a child is ready to be told about sex? about the dangers of going with a stranger? about divorce?

Have you ever heard these phrases?

kicked the bucket   passed away   gone to live with Jesus

Why do you think people find it so difficult to use the words 'death', 'dying' or 'dead'?

We call phrases such as 'passed away' **euphemisms**: phrases which wrap up unpleasant facts in flowery words. What other euphemisms have you come across?

See if you can explain what 'reading between the lines' means.

In this poem, Carole Satyamuri describes words as 'dust-sheets', and 'blinds'. Think about how words could be dust-sheets or blinds.

Between the Lines

Words were dust-sheets, blinds.
People dying randomly, for 'want of breath',
shadowed my bed-times.
Babies happened;
adults buried questions under bushes.

Nouns would have been too robust
for body-parts; they were
curt, homeless prepositions - 'inside',
'down there', 'behind', 'below'. No word
for what went on in darkness, overheard.

Underground, straining for language
that would let me out, I pressed to the radio,
read forbidden books. And once
visited Mr Cole. His seventeen
budgerigars praised God continually.

randomly – for no reason
shadowed my bed-times – made me worry at night

robust – bold

curt – abrupt

He loved all words, he said, though he used
few to force a kiss. All that summer
I longed to ask my mother, starved myself,
prayed, imagined skirts were getting tight,
hoped jumping down ten stairs would put it right.

My parents fought in other rooms,
their tight-lipped murmuring muffled
by flock wallpaper.
What was wrong, what they had to say
couldn't be shared with me.

He crossed the threshold in a wordless   **threshold** – entrance
slam of doors. 'Gone to live near work'
my mother said, before she tracked down
my diary, broke the lock, made me cut out
pages that guessed what silence was about.

Carole Satyamuri

THINKING/TALKING POINTS

◆ What sort of home and upbringing do you think that this girl had?
   How do you imagine her parents? Which details give you that
   impression?

◆ 'Babies happened', 'adults buried questions under bushes'
   What do you understand by these phrases?

◆ Who was Mr Cole? Why do you think the girl couldn't tell her
   mother what he had done?

◆ 'He crossed the threshold in a wordless slam of doors.' What do you
   imagine happening here? Try describing the scene as it takes place.

◆ What do you think of the mother's behaviour at the end? Give your
   reasons.

Now read through the poem again a couple of times to see what else
needs thinking about before choosing your assignment.

ROLE-PLAY

▶ *In pairs*

Improvise the conversation that takes place between this girl and a teacher/social worker or friend about what's happening at home.

Improvise the scene which takes place when the mother finds the girl's diary.

Think about the reasons that the mother might give her daughter for wanting her to destroy certain pages. What do you think the girl might say about her mother looking in her diary in the first place?

You may like to end your scene with the mother and daughter trying to talk about some of the things they have been keeping from each other.

ASSIGNMENT

▶ *On your own*

Either: Using the details in the poem but adding lots of your own ideas, try writing two or three of the girl's diary entries for the week leading up to her father's departure.

The girl 'guessed what silence was about' in her diary. Try to capture the loneliness, fear and confusion that she feels about all that's been happening.

Or: Write your own story called 'Between the Lines'. You might wish to use the same situation of a marriage break-up or think of another situation in which some parents try to keep their child/children in the dark about something.

13 Narrative writing (ii)

▶ On your own or whole class

Read through this poem a few times. Experiment with different ways of reading it.

Then read through the opening of *Metamorphosis*, a short story by Franz Kafka.

Brer Nancy

Flamboyant spider-man,
Spiralled sagaciously
In his web
On a cradling calabash-tree;
Strutting on the freckled corpses
Of moth and lizard,
And the wind-blown guts
Of a bumble-bee.
His fragile pot-belly,
Full of laughter;
Conjuring sorceric folklore,
Intuitive
In the magic of his living.

Faustin Charles

Metamorphosis

As Gregor Samsa awoke one morning from uneasy dreams, he found himself transformed in his bed into a gigantic insect. He was lying on his hard, armour-plated back. When he lifted his head a little he could see his dome-like brown belly divided into stiff arched segments. The bed-quilt could hardly keep in position; it was about to slide off completely. His numerous legs were pitifully thin compared to the rest of his bulk. They waved helplessly before his eyes...

ASSIGNMENT

Draw a picture suggested by the poem.

ASSIGNMENT

Choose one of the following episodes to write. You may like to write as if you are Gregor describing what happens:

1   You are stranded, a huge beetle on its back. Your legs are waving in the air; you are in danger of falling heavily off the bed onto the floor. You are frightened that you might hurt yourself.
Are you hungry? Thirsty? Cold? Confused?
Does what has happened to you make any sense at all?
What/who could be responsible for your transformation?

2   You are helpless: you decide to call for somebody: father? sister? neighbour?
Do you still have a human voice? When you try to speak, what sounds come out?
Does anyone come to help? How does s/he react when s/he opens the door?

3   You decide to try to get off the bed without calling for help. How do you manage to turn? What does that feel like? How are you able to work your new body so that you can explore the room as a huge insect might?

What does it feel like inside this new body? To have so many tiny legs and a hard shell?

What can you see? Colours, shapes? Can you see more or less than you could through human eyes?

Are your hearing/sense of smell/sense of touch/sense of taste more or less acute than they were when you were a person? How does the familiar room appear from an insect's point of view?

Are any of the human things in the room beginning to appear strange? Useless? Do you find anything in the room which a human wouldn't have noticed but which as an insect you have to explore?

4 To begin with, your transformation is not complete. You can still talk and think in human ways, still enjoy human food and human company.

Most of your family and friends, once they get over their shock, try to treat you kindly, hoping the change will not be for ever.

As time passes, however, you find your human self changing into a new insect self. You begin to see the world differently from the way people see it. You develop new interests, new fears, new needs and it becomes harder to talk in human language. You hear, see, sense things which your visitors are not aware of. They talk about things you don't remember or can't understand.

Gradually you feel people losing interest in you or becoming disgusted with or frightened of you. Or simply bored.

ASSIGNMENT

Choose a creature which you find fascinating, for example:

    a snake   a hawk   a spider   a rat   a whale . . .

Imagine being that creature, looking through its eyes, living in its habitat, having its feelings.

Write a short story about the day in which you were mysteriously changed from being you into being that creature.

Describe your changing feelings and the way things gradually looked, sounded, smelt, felt and tasted differently.

What are the best things about being this creature? And the worst?

FOLLOW UP

Have a look at one or two of these:

Roald Dahl	*Royal Jelly*
H G Wells	*The Valley of Spiders*
Thom Gunn	*Considering the Snail*
Wilfred Owen	*Disabled; Mental Cases*
Gerard Manley Hopkins	*The Windhover*
Ted Hughes	*Wodwo; Hawk Roosting*

14 Talkshop (ii)

▶ *In pairs*

You enter a theatre. On stage the lights are already up; there are no curtains - just an empty stage set with a few props.

Discuss how the opening scene of a play might develop around each of these sets.

ROLE·PLAY

Now choose just one of the sets and improvise the opening scene of a play involving only as many characters as the two of you can easily play. (One of you may go off as one character and then come on as somebody else.)

Mime, using any of the the props which will help your scene to develop but do not feel you have to use them all (or any).

▶ *In pairs*

Read this this poem through a few times, taking it in turns to read each complete sentence.

Conversation Piece

By moonlight
At midnight,
Under the vines,
A hotel chair
Settles down moodily before the headlines
Of a still-folded evening newspaper.

The other chair
Of the pair
Lies on its back,
Stiff as in pain,
Having been overturned with an angry crack;
And there till morning, alas, it must remain.

On the terrace
No blood-trace,
No sorry glitter
Of a knife, nothing:
Not even the fine-torn fragments of a letter
Or the dull gleam of a flung-off wedding-ring.

Still stable
On the table
Two long-stemmed glasses,
One full of drink,
Watch how the rat among the vines passes
And how the moon trembles on the crag's brink.

Robert Graves

THINKING/TALKING POINTS

Work together on making a sketch of the scene the poem describes, in a similar style to the ones on pages 46–47.

Looking at all the evidence in the poem, what can you suggest happened to leave things as the poet describes them? Use your imagination to replay the scene.

Here are some things to consider:

◆ How many people/animals do you think may have been there?

◆ What do you think each of them looked like? How old were they? How were they dressed? Why were they there?

◆ What were they doing, saying?

◆ What sorts of voices do you imagine?

◆ What mood do you think the people were in?

◆ How might the chair have been overturned? Why?

◆ How did the scene end?

When you have discussed various scenarios, improvise a scene which ends with the props arranged as the poem describes them.

You may like to write up your scene as a playscript.

▶ *On your own or in small groups*
Read this extract from Thea von Harbou's novel *Metropolis*:

Freeze-Frame (i)

The girl walked through the passages that were so familiar to her. The bright little lamp in her hand roved over the roof of stone and over the stone walls, where, in niches, the thousand-year-old dead slept.

The girl had never known fear of the dead; only reverence and gravity in face of their gravity. Today she saw neither wall nor dead. She walked on, smiling and not knowing she did it. She felt like singing. With an expression of happiness, which was still incredulous and yet complete, she said the name of her beloved over to herself.

Quite softly: 'Freder . . .' And once more: 'Freder . . .'
Then she raised her head, listening attentively, standing quite still. It came back as a whisper. An echo? No.
Almost inaudibly a word was breathed:
'Maria . . .'

She turned around, blissfully startled. Was it possible that he had come back?
'Freder!' she called. She listened.
No answer.
'Freder . . .!'

Nothing.

But suddenly there came a cool draught of air which made the hair on her neck quiver, and a hand of snow ran down her back. There came an agonised sigh - a sigh which would not come to an end . . .

The girl stood still. The bright little lamp which she held in her hand let its gleam play tremblingly about her feet.
'Freder . . .?
Now her voice too was only a whisper.

No answer. But behind her, in the depths of the passage she would have to pass through, a gentle gliding slink became perceptible: feet in soft shoes on rough stones.

THINKING/TALKING POINTS

How do you imagine the place where this scene takes place? If you were turning it into a film, what sort of location would you choose? What would the lighting be like? What kind of atmosphere would you try to create? What music/sound-effects would you use?

How do you imagine Maria? Young? Old? Thin? Plump? Dark? Fair? Strong? Weak? . . . Describe the way you imagine her hair, her eyes, the clothes she is wearing.

What sort of story do you think *Metropolis* might be, judging just from this extract? Who/What do you think 'Metropolis' might be/might mean? What sort of country/town do you think the story happens in? When might the story be set? Today? A thousand years ago?

Suggest why Maria is walking down the passage. Where has she been? Where might she be heading?

Suggest as many different ways as you can that the story might continue.

ASSIGNMENT

See if you can write just two or three more paragraphs which follow on from this extract. Try to write in a similar style so a new reader would not guess where the original ended and your bit began. Do not try to 'finish' the story.

When everyone has written their sequels, you may like to read them to each other or make them into a display.

16 Shaping a story (ii)

Freeze-Frame (ii)

1

2

3

4

THINKING/TALKING POINTS

▶ *In pairs or small groups*

Look at the photographs on pages 52 and 53. Imagine that each of them records a moment in a story.

Take it in turns to describe exactly what you think is happening in each picture.
Whereabouts is it happening? At what time of day? Is it warm or cold? Is the sky cloudy or clear?
What do you think are the most important details in each picture?
What mood/atmosphere does the picture suggest to you?

> *joy despair anger loneliness greed friendship*
> *sadness anxiety panic business terror relief . . .*

Now discuss just one of the pictures.

Decide together on where and when the scene takes place. Discuss what the camera might see if it moved a little to the right, to the left, above and below the scene we see.

Suggest some things which might have been happening a few minutes before that snapshot was taken, for example:

◆ Who parked the car there? What was s/he wearing? Carrying? Was s/he alone? Where is s/he now?

◆ Where/what/who is the girl running from? Why?

◆ What are the men talking about? What are they planning to do next?

◆ What kind of place is the boy in? How did he get there?

See how many alternatives you can come up with.

Now discuss which of the suggestions is the most interesting. Which one could you develop into a gripping story?

WRITER'S WORKSHOP

Working on your own or in a group, plan a brief extract from a story around **one** of the pictures.

What might happen next? Will other things/people enter the scene? If a movie camera were to record what happened in the next ten minutes, what would it see? What would a microphone hear?

You may like to set out your ideas as a story board, something like this:

PHOTOGRAPH 1 (Men in café)

Or as a written plan something like this:

PHOTOGRAPH 3 (Boy behind bars)

◆ Harsh voice heard: 'No use you staring. No one will ever find you here.'

◆ Boy turns to peer through bars, not noticing a figure moving behind him.

◆ Boy's face lights up as he notices something/someone across the street.

◆ The sound of brakes squealing . . .

Experiment with lots of ways the story might go until you have found a series of incidents which flow smoothly and hold the reader's interest.

ASSIGNMENT

Now turn your storyboard or plan into a narrative. It should read like an **extract** from a longer story, rather like the extract you read from *Metropolis* in Unit 15.

Remember, you do not have to explain everything which happened a long time before the picture you chose was taken. And you are not going to end the story. What you are trying to do is write an exciting, dramatic, colourful fragment, which reads as if it comes from a film or a novel.

▶ *In small groups*

Here is an extract from Dickens's novel, *Dombey & Son*. Read it together:

Disaster!

The first shock of a great earthquake had rent the whole neighbourhood to its centre. Traces of its course were visible on every side. Houses were knocked down; streets broken through and stopped; deep pits and trenches dug in the ground; enormous heaps of earth and clay thrown up; buildings that were undermined and shaking, propped by great beams of wood. Here, a chaos of carts, overthrown and jumbled together, lay topsy-turvy at the bottom of a steep unnatural hill; there, confused treasures of iron soaked and rusted in something that had accidentally become a pond. Everywhere were bridges that led nowhere; thoroughfares that were wholly impassable; Babel towers of chimneys, wanting half their height; temporary wooden houses and enclosures, in the most unlikely situations; carcasses of ragged tenements, and fragments of unfinished walls and arches, and piles of scaffolding, and wildernesses of bricks, and giant forms of cranes, and tripods straddling above nothing.

There were a hundred thousand shapes and substances of incompleteness, wildly mingled out of their places, upside down, burrowing in the earth, aspiring in the air, mouldering in the water, and unintelligible as any dream.

Hot springs and fiery eruptions, the usual attendants upon earthquakes, lent their contributions of confusions to the scene. Boiling water hissed and heaved within dilapidated walls, whence, also, the glare and roar of flames came issuing forth; and mounds of ashes blocked up rights of way, and wholly changed the law and custom of the neighbourhood.

ASSIGNMENT

Flood FIRE Famine ha

Pestilence s HURRICANE CH

Earthquake Avalanche Kill

Every now and again, the world is stopped short by news of a disaster: human suffering on such a scale that everyday worries about acne and haircuts, soap powder and share prices seem ridiculously trivial.

Imagine something catastrophic happening in the area where you live. It might be a freak of Nature – such as a hurricane or a boiling heat wave. Or it might be some one-in-a-hundred-thousand chance – such as a jumbo jet or a huge meteorite crashing to earth.

Perhaps the possibilities of such a disaster are always present in your neighbourhood? A factory which manufactures toxic chemicals which might catch fire? A nuclear power plant which could develop a dangerous leak? A dam which could burst? A railway where there might be a dreadful collision?

What we want you to do is write a short narrative in which taken-for-granted everyday normality is suddenly shattered and a very familiar safe place suddenly becomes a nightmarish landscape.

Stage 1
The first couple of paragraphs should create a sense of calm, of predictable dullness: perhaps two friends talking about what they watched on television last night. Or what they plan to do at the weekend.

Fit in a few descriptive details of the city/town/village so that the reader gets a strong impression of how it usually looks, sounds, feels . . . Here's an example:

> It was a warm Tuesday afternoon and Joan decided to take her three year old, Suzi, to the swings. They trotted down the High Street and stopped to buy an ice cream. 'Lovely day. Been busy?'

Stage 2

Then disaster strikes. Make this stage very brief, full of the necessary information, for example:

> Mr Higgins, the power-station supervisor, noticed too late that not one but three red warning lamps were flashing. There was a crack and then an explosion followed by the roar of escaping, radioactive steam.

Or:

> What had been a downpour was now a wild tempest, tumbling cars over and throwing people around like confetti at a wedding.

Stage 3

The main part of the narrative should come now: a description of the place you described at the beginning but almost unrecognisable in a chaos of movement, wreckage, panic and weird sights, sounds and smells.

Think how particular places you know might look if such a disaster struck. Where emergency help might have to come from. How people would behave in the first few minutes' confusion.

Don't try to 'end' the story. The power of the piece will come from the contrast between the picture you painted at the beginning and what you describe at the end.

You may like to illustrate your writing.

18 Autobiography (i)

▶ *On your own*

Here's a piece written by Mark Maplethorpe when he was sixteen. It has vivid characters, a strong sense of place and a shape to it we could call a plot. But what makes the story strong is that it feels authentic – a person simply telling about something which mattered to him.

The Threepenny Tip

It was near the end of the round. I leant the old paper-bike against the house wall and went round the back. It was a typical council house. The back fence hadn't seen creosote in years. I knocked on the tall gate. The dog inside started barking.

'Coming! Shut up, Rusty! Get down!'

The old woman opened the gate.

'Cold morning, isn't it?' I said.

'Yes,' she sighed. She shut the gate.

The yard wasn't big, so the dog was always trying to get out. They had built a rough old shed next to the outside toilet. They used it for the dog's kennel and to keep the old man's wheelchair dry.

We went in the kitchen. It stunk of the Sunday dinner. It was a small, dank kitchen. An old, large, enamelled gas stove boiled something on the top in an old brown saucepan. She opened another door and we went into the living room. The old man, as usual, was sitting in front of the fire. I handed him his *Sunday Mirror*.

'Got any shillings this week, luv?' she asked.

'Yes, I think so.' I gave her the *News of The World* and emptied my money on the grubby-white tablecloth. She paid for the papers and slipped a threepenny bit over to me. I looked her in the eyes, as if to say no thank you. She passed me a ten-shilling note. I gave her ten shilling pieces.

'Thank you,' she said and put them in her purse.

I put my money back into the bag. She spent most of her money on keeping the house warm. If her husband got cold, it would make him cough. He had progressive lung cancer.

I gazed around the living room as she spoke. The mantlepiece was an array of pictures and ornaments. In the middle was an old clock with Roman pillars and a pediment over the top. It didn't go, it was stuck on ten past three. The battered settee, with newspaper on the seats, was in front of the fire. The old man always sat there. Behind him was the sideboard. This, too, was covered in pictures and curios and another clock. This one did work, but was always five minutes fast. I glanced down at the floor; it had a grubby, brown carpet, well-worn, no doubt a wedding present. The room smelt of the cooking in the kitchen. It lingered about and smeared the windows. As I sat at the table opposite the window, I noticed the crumbs on the tablecloth which had been left over from breakfast.

The old man put on his glasses. He never said much. I'd say he was about seventy-one. I could only guess on his height, as I had never seen him standing up. I knew he could hardly walk, though he always had a walking stick near him. He wore the same scrubby, black jacket and cap all the time. He always wore a shirt without a collar. I think he did this so as to breathe easier. He was virtually bald, but he had a few strands of white hair. He wore a small moustache, which covered a part of that face. It was blotchy and heavily wrinkled. His giant eyes loomed up through his extra-strong glasses. He held his paper in his large, weak hands. He started coughing and wheezing. His wife stopped talking for a moment. Then started again. The old man was a pathetic wreck. I just had to look away from him.

There were many times I wish, I wished I'd had not been there. The old man could not use the outside toilet. So, being poor, he used a jam jar in his lap. For weeks, I wondered why he used to groan and flinch when he had a towel on his lap. He was embarrassed and hurt when I noticed. It was as bad as the time when he tried to get up and reach the paper and fell down.

The mongrel dog jumped up.

'Get down, Rusty!' shouted the old woman. The old man said something too, but I couldn't understand what he said. Each week he used to cough more often and the nurse came more often too. He began to lose weight.

His cheeks fell in. His face became hideous. The coughing fits lasted longer and they were terrible to listen to. I found that I was glad to get away. Then, one week, when I went in, he was not there.

'Where's the old . . . er, your husband?'

'He . . .' She broke off and looked at the settee. 'He died on Thursday.'

I couldn't speak, even if I'd wanted to.

'*News of The World* only, please.' She gave me the money. I put it in my bag. 'Any shilli . . .'

'No shillings,' she said.

Then she handed me that threepenny tip.

I could have cried.

Mark Maplethorpe

THINKING/TALKING POINTS

The ingredients of Mark's story are simple: the newspaper round; the old couple; the dog and their house; the old man's progressive lung cancer. The descriptive details are there because they help to bring everything to life – sights, smells, sounds. The dialogue is simple and sounds like what real people say – not like something made up for the sake of 'characterisation' or 'plot'.

What holds it together is the story-teller's straightforward honest feelings: he just says how he felt, without trying to pretend.

ASSIGNMENT

Write about a family you knew when you were younger – a family you visited now and again.

Try to remember how it felt as you approached the house and what it was that gave you those feelings – the way the curtains hung, the colour of the walls, the smell in the hallway, the noise of the radio, the kitchen furniture, the lighting, the way you were greeted . . .

See if you can recapture the way the family spoke, behaved - the little things which helped to make them special – the ornaments on the window sill, the way they made tea, their pets, their interests, the sorts of questions they'd ask you . . .

Don't worry too much about plot: your family doesn't have to go through a crisis – maybe you simply moved away from each other or had a row over something trivial and lost touch.

See if in a few paragraphs, you can convey to somebody who never knew them as strong a picture of that family you once knew as Mark Maplethorpe has given you of the old couple in his story.

19 Short story workshop (ii)

It Must Be Different

Sylvia Weeks and Max Porter had known each other five months, but she never took him home to her place till that autumn evening when they had walked in the streets after the show, and the rain had begun to fall.

It had started when Max began suddenly to tell her that there was a real chance for him to get along in the radio business, and then her heart had begun to beat unevenly, for she became aware that he was getting ready to talk about wanting to marry her. He was so simple and honest about it, that she became humble and shy, and they walked along silently, both anxious about what was to be said; and then the rain began to fall in large heavy drops. Ducking their heads, they ran along the street hand in hand and stood breathless on the stoop outside her place, watching the wet pavement shining under the street light.   **stoop** – porch

Sylvia could not bear to let him go as he had gone on other nights; it was as though they had looked for each other for months, and had now met suddenly face to face. That magical feeling was still flowing between them, and she couldn't bear to let him go until all the necessary words had been said, or the things done that would hold them together forever.

'Come on in for a little while, Max,' she said.

'Are you sure it'll be all right?'

'I think they'll be in bed,' she said.

They laughed a little while Sylvia fumbled in her purse for   **purse** – handbag
her latchkey; then they tried to go in quietly. When they were in the hall, they heard someone coughing in the livingroom. Sylvia whispered uneasily: 'I thought they'd be in bed.'

'Maybe I'd better not come in,' he said.

'Come on, anyway,' she said.

In the living room Sylvia's mother, a large woman with a face that had been quite pretty once, but which was now soft and heavy, was standing with an alarm clock in her hand. She was on her way to bed, and she had been urging her husband, who still sat in an armchair in his shirt-sleeves and suspenders reading the paper, to go along with her, so he wouldn't disturb her later on. When Sylvia came in with Max following shyly, the mother was flustered and began to tidy her grey hair with her hand. 'We were on our way to bed. We were just waiting for you, Sylvia,' she said reproachfully.

'We wanted to walk after the show, Mother; but it rained. This is Max, Mother,' Sylvia said.

'Oh, hello, Max. We've heard about you.'

'If it's too late, I won't stay, Mrs Weeks.'

'So you're Max, eh,' the father said, getting up. He was a furniture-maker who worked hard all day, and who usually hurried out of the room when a visitor came in the evening; but now he stood there staring at Max as if he had been wondering about him a long time.

And Mrs Weeks, looking at Sylvia, said: 'You must have been having a good time, dear. You look happy and kind of excited.'

'I'm not excited. I was just hurrying in the rain,' Sylvia said.

'I guess it's just the rain and hurrying that makes your eyes shine,' the mother said; but the free ecstatic eagerness she saw in her daughter's face worried her, and her glance was troubled as she tried to make her husband notice that Sylvia's face glowed with some secret delight that had come out of being with this boy, who was a stranger and might not be trustworthy. Sylvia and Max were standing underneath the light, and Sylvia with her flushed cheeks and her dark head seemed more marvellously eager than ever before. It was easy for them to feel the restlessness and the glowing warmth in her, and the love she had been giving; and then the mother and father, looking at Max, who seemed very boyish with his rain-wet hair shining under the light, smiled a little, not wanting to be hostile, yet feeling sure that Sylvia and this boy had touched some new intimacy that night.

In a coaxing, worried voice Mrs Weeks said: 'Now don't stay up late, Sylvia darling, will you?' Again her husband's eyes met hers in that thoughtful, uneasy way; then they said pleasantly: 'Goodnight, Max. We're glad to meet you. Good night, Sylvia.' And then they went to bed.

When they had gone, Max said: 'They certainly made that pretty clear, didn't they?'

'Made what clear?'

'That they wouldn't trust me alone with my grandmother.'

'They didn't say anything at all, Max.'

'Didn't you see how they stared at me? I'll bet they're listening now.'

'Is that why you're whispering?'

'Sure. They expect us to whisper, don't they?'

They sat down on the couch, but they both felt that if they caressed each other, or became gentle and tender, they were only making a beginning at something that was expected of them by the mother and father going to bed in the next room. So they were awkward and uneasy with each other. They felt like strangers. When he put his arm on her shoulder, it lay there heavy, and they were silent, listening to the rain falling outside.

Then there was a sound in the hall, the sound of shuffling slippers, and when they looked up quickly, they saw a bit of the mother's dressing-gown sweeping past the door. Then the slippers were still. In a little while there was a worried, hesitant shuffling; then they came back again past the door.

hesitant – shy

'Did you want something, Mother?' Sylvia called.

'No, nothing,' the mother said, looking in. She tried to smile, but she was a little ashamed, and she would not look directly at Sylvia. 'I couldn't get to sleep,' she said.

'Aren't you feeling well?'

'I lie awake, you know. I hear every sound in here. I might just as well be in the room with you, I guess.' And then with that half-ashamed droop of her head, she shuffled away again.

'Is she policing us?' Max asked irritably.

'I think she's just not feeling well,' Sylvia said.

They both sat stiffly, listening, though she wanted to put her cheek down on Max's shoulder. In a little while they heard the murmur of voices in the bedroom; and Sylvia knew that her father and mother were lying awake worrying about her. Out of their own memories, out of everything that had happened to them, they felt sure they knew what would be happening to her. The murmuring voices rose a little; the sounds were short and sharp as the mother and father wrangled and worried and felt helpless. And Sylvia, trying hard to recover those moments she had thought so beautiful, hurrying along the street with Max, knew that it was no use, and that they were gone, and she felt miserable.

wrangled – argued

'I think I'll get out,' Max whispered.

'Please don't go now,' she coaxed. 'It's the first night we've felt like this. Please stay.'

She wanted to soothe the hate and contempt out of him by rubbing her fingers through his hair; yet she only sat beside him stiffly, waiting, while the house grew silent, for warmth and eagerness to come again. It was so silent she thought she could hear the beating of his heart. She was ashamed to whisper. Max kept stirring uneasily, wanting to go.

Then they were startled by the father's voice calling roughly: 'Sylvia!'

'What is it?' she said.

'What's keeping you there? Why are you so quiet? What are you doing?'

'Nothing.'

'It's getting late,' he called.

She knew her father must have tried hard to stop himself calling out like that; yet she felt so humiliated she could not look at Max.

'I'm getting out quick,' Max said.

'All right. But it's nothing; he's just worrying,' she pleaded.

'They've been lying in bed all the time listening.'

'They're very fond of me,' she said. 'They'd do it, no matter what it was.'

But hating the house and her people, he snapped at her, 'Why don't they put a padlock on you?'

Then she felt that the feeling that had been so good between them, that she had tried to bring into the house and bring into her own life, could not last here, that his voice would never grow shy and hesitant as he fumbled for a few words here, that this was really what she was accustomed to, and it was not good. She began to cry softly. 'Don't be sore, Max,' she said.

'I'm not sore at you.'

'They felt pretty sure they know how it goes; that's all,' she pleaded with him. 'They think it'll have to go with me the way it went with them.'

'That's pretty plain.'

'I don't think either one of them want to see me get married. Nothing ever happened the right way for them. I can remember ever since I was a kid.'

'Remember what?'

'They never felt sure of each other. They parted once, and even now when they get mad, they're suspicious of each other and wouldn't trust each other around the block. But that was years go, really,' she said, holding him tightly by the arm, and pleading that he understand the life in her home was not loose and unhappy. 'They're both very fond of me,' she said apologetically. 'They've had a tough time all their lives. We've been pretty poor, and – well – they worry about me; that's all.'

Her eyes looked so scared that Max was afraid to question her, and they stood together thinking of the mother and father lying awake in the bedroom.

'I guess they feel that way about people, out of what's happened to them, eh?' he said.

'That's it.'

'Their life doesn't have to be your life, does it?'

accustomed to – used to

sore – cross

mad – angry

apologetically – making excuses

'It certainly doesn't,' she said, and she was full of relief, for she knew by his face that the things she had blurted out hadn't disturbed him at all.

'I wrote my people about you,' he said. 'They want to see you. I sent them a snapshot.'

'That was a very bad one; I look terrible in it.'

'Can you get your holidays in August, Sylvia?'

'I think so. I'll ask a long time ahead.'

'We'll go to the country and see my folks. I swear you'll like them,' he said.

That moment at the door was the one fine free moment they had had since coming in, and it did not seem to belong to anything that had happened in the house that night. While they held each other, whispering, 'Good-bye, good-bye,' they were sure they would always be gentle and faithful, and their life together would be good. Then they laughed softly, knowing they were sharing the same secret contempt for the wisdom of her people.

Without waiting to hear the sound of his footfalls outside, she rushed resolutely to her mother's bedroom and turned on the light, and called sharply: 'Mother.'

But her mother and father, who were lying with their heads together on the pillow, did not stir, and Sylvia said savagely: 'Wake up – do you hear? I was never so ashamed in my life.'

One of her father's thin arms hung loose over the side of the bed, the wrinkled hand drooping from the wrist, and his shoulders were half uncovered. Her mother was breathing irregularly with her mouth open a little, as though her dreams too were troubled. They looked very tired, and Sylvia wavered.

Then her father stirred, and his blue eyes opened and blinked, and he mumbled sleepily: 'Is that you, Sylvia?'

'Yes,' she said.

'All right. Turn out the light,' he said, and he closed his eyes.

Yet she still stood there, muttering hesitantly to herself: 'It's just that I don't want to get to feel the way you do about people.'

Then she grew frightened, for the two faces on the pillow now seemed like the faces of two tired people who had worked hard all their lives, and had grown old together; and her own life had been simply a part of theirs, a part of whatever had happened to them. Still watching the two faces, she began to long with all her soul that her own love and her hope would be strong enough to resist the things that had happened to them. 'It'll be different with me and Max. It must be different,' she muttered.

But as she heard only their irregular breathing, her fright grew. The whole of her life ahead seemed to become uncertain, and her happiness with Max so terribly insecure.

Morley Callaghan

blurted out – said in a rush

footfalls – footsteps
resolutely – boldly

wavered – hesitated

ASSIGNMENT

Either: Write the conversation which you think Sylvia's mother and father were having in the bedroom whilst the young couple were in the living room. Try to bring out not only how they feel about Sylvia and about Max but how their own relationship makes it difficult for them to trust the young couple.

Or: Write a sequel to Morley Callaghan's story. You could call it 'It had to be Different'. What happens when Sylvia visits Max's folks? Is it a very different atmosphere from the one in her home? Are there tensions there too?
You may like to write in a similar style to the story or choose to write as if Sylvia were telling a friend about it.

Or: Write your own story about someone (perhaps yourself) taking somebody home for the first time. Try to bring out the subtle ways in which everyone's behaviour is just a little different from usual. Your story doesn't have to be grim – you may want to make it funny! Maybe the title 'Meet my Folks!' would fit your story.

20 Poetry workshop (iv)

▶

In pairs

Here is a poem which explores the relationship between a man and wife. Some of the key words in the poem have been deleted.

Discuss the poem and suggest what you think are the best words to fill the gaps.

Her Husband

Comes home .... with coal-dust deliberately
To grime the sink and foul towels and let her
Learn with .... brush and scrubbing board
The .... character of money.

And let her learn through what kind of dust
He has .... his thirst and the right to quench it
And what sweat he has exchanged for his ....
And the blood-weight of money. He'll humble her

With new light on her ....
The fried, woody chips, kept .... two hours in the oven,
Are only part of her answer.
Hearing the rest, he .... them to the fire back

And is away round the house-end singing
'Come back to Sorrento' in a ....
Of resounding corrugated iron.
Her back has bunched into a .... as an insult.

For .... will have their rights.
Their jurors are to be assembled
From the little crumbs of soot. Their brief
Goes straight up to .... and .... more is heard of it.

Ted Hughes

A complete version of this poem can be found on p.101.

THINKING/TALKING POINTS

◆ What impression do you have of the husband? Which of these words do you think describe him?

> *hard-working   loyal   caring   brutal   strong   brave   sensitive*
> *proud   callous   selfish   decent   arrogant   indifferent*
> *easy-going   manly   decent   healthy   ambitious   lonely*
> *cocky   weak   cruel   independent   old   jolly*

Add some new words of your own to any you have chosen.

◆ How would you describe the wife and her situation? Would you pick any of these words to describe them?

> *normal   helpless   feeble   tragic   predictable   lonely   sad*
> *ugly   homely   angry   isolated   tense   routine   abused*
> *her own fault   useless   resentful   resigned   bitter   hopeful*

◆ What do you think the poet's attitude is to the situation he is describing?

FOR DISCUSSION

When you have worked out a version of the poem which you are pleased with, join another pair and compare what each of you has come up with.

Discuss each other's choices of words and the different impressions you have created of the man, his wife and their situation.

ASSIGNMENT

You may decide to produce a further version of the poem, combining the best features you have come up with.

Either: Write out your version of the poem and explain why you have chosen the words you have to fill the gaps. Are there any spaces which you found particularly difficult to fill?

Or: Use the poem as the starting point for a piece of writing in which the miner's wife describes a typical day in her life. You could call it 'My Husband'.

Begin with her alone, expecting her husband home. Then describe the episode in the poem as you think the woman would have experienced it.

End with the wife's thoughts after her husband has left.

▶ *Inpairs*

takeitinturnstoreadthroughthis

firstofallwhatdoyouwanttodowewanttowriteaplaywriteaplaynowewan
ttowriteastorytheywanttowriteaplayyeswewanttowriteaplayaboutsome
kidswhobreakintothisoldfactoryrubbishourideasmuchbetterwhosaid
thatwhatoneatatime

wewanttowriteaplay

andwewanttowriteastory

whydontyougetonwithit

becausewhenwewriteitoutnoonecanreadit

icanreadit

butonlyslowly

whatstheproblem

everythingsjumbledupandyoucanttellhowtosaythingssuchasgoi
nghome

why

wedontknowifthatssomeonesayingimgoinghomeorsomeoneaskingareyo
ugoinghome

whynotuseaquestionmark?

thatsokforquestionsbuthowdoyouknowifsomeonesangryorexcited?
useanexclamationmarkbirdbrain!

sothatswhattheyrefor!

stilllooksajumbletomehowdoyouknowwhentotakeabreaththissentencei
skillingmeandimstillonlyhalfwaythrough

well, ifyouneedabreather, thenuseacomma.

andifyouneedalongerbreak, useafullstop.

itsbetter, butitsstillnotright,imsure.

butatleastitseasiertoseewhichwordsbelongtogether.

butwhenwearetalkingsaidjanice,lookingpuzzled,
weneedtoshowwhichwordssomeoneactuallysays,andwhichwordsaretell
ingthestory, fillinginthebackground.howdoyoudothat?

"likethis,ofcourse,"saidpeter, whowasalwaysshowingoff.

"swot!"shoutedjimmy.

"creep!" hissedsally.

"yourejustjealousofmysuperioreducation!"saidpeter,underhisbreath.

"sowhatsallthefussabout?youmightaswellgetonwithyourstory!"saidth
eteacher.

"wewanttowriteaplay,"screamedellen.

"noastoryaboutsomerunawayhorses!"yelledmiriam.

"shutup!oneatatime!"

"youmeanstartanewlineeachtimesomeonenewstartstospeak?"

"precisely."

"evenifitsjustoneword?"

"precisely."

everyoneheavedasighofrelief.

"ourstorysallaboutthepigs."

"yousaiditwasaboutagang!"

"yes,thepigs.theyrecalledthepigs!"

"oh,youmeanThePigs!"

"youwhat?"

"ThePigs,toshowitsaname."

"whataboutpeter?"

"youmeanPeter?"

"isee."

"begyourpardon?"

"Isee."

"useacapitalletterforanameandforI."

"precisely. goon."

"Ibegyourpardon?ohIseewhatyoumean.well,thisgang,ThePigs,break intoanoldfactoryontheedgeofarubbishdumpinLondonsomewhere."

"IthoughttheylivedonBlackIsland?"

"wewrotethatonewhenyouwereaway,Jeremy!"

"apostrophes!"squeakedCatherine.

"blessyou,dear."

"apostrophes!"sheinsisted.

"Ibegyourpardon?"

"apostrophes!whataboutapostrophes?"

"whataboutthem?"

"apostrophes!youresupposedtouseapostrophes!"therewasnostopping Catherineonceshegotanideaintoherbrain.

"why?"

"toshowyouvebeentoschool."

"li'ke'th'is?"

"ye'sallo'verth'eplaceande'speciallyw'he'nt'here's'an'sIb'elieve."

"look'same'sstome."

"no!youdon'tusethemunlessthey'reneeded!"

"wherethen?"

"that'swhen."

"whenyou'vemissedoutaletter?"

"that'sit!"

"what'stheproblem?"

"noproblem.theonlyruleaboutapostrophesis,
whenindoubt,leave'emout."

"whataboutwithans?"

"onlyuseanapostrophewithstoshowsomethingbelongs."

"likeJane'shairstyle?"

"it'sdreadful.yes,Jane'shairstyle.that'swhereyouneedanapostrophe."

"Philip'shangover,Mark'sbignose,theteacher'sappallinglackofstyle."

"precisely.well, nowyouknowallaboutpunctuation,
whynotwriteyourplay?"

"novel,actually."

"Justonemorething."

"comeagain?"

"Justonemorething.Incaseanyonehadn'tnoticed.Idon'twanttotakeal
ldayoverthis.Anyonecaughtonyet?"

"Showwhereanewsentencebeginsbyusingacapitalletter."

"Precisely."

"Easy,isn'tit?"

"O.K. Getonwithyourwork."

"Rightthen.ButI'msurethere'sstillsomethingnotquiteright."

ASSIGNMENT

When you've worked out the sense of this piece, try writing out the first
two pages so they're easy to read quickly.

22 ▌ Autobiography (ii)

In this extract from her autobiography, Jean Rhys remembers her early years in Dominica in the Caribbean:

Smile Please

Now it is time to talk about Meta, my nurse and the terror of my life. She had been there ever since I could remember: a short, stocky woman, very black and always, I thought, in a bad temper.

I never saw Meta smile. She always seemed to be brooding over some terrible, unforgettable wrong. When I wasn't old enough to walk by myself I can remember the feel of her hard hand as she hauled me along to the Botanical Gardens where she was supposed to take me every afternoon. She walked so fast that I had to run to keep up with her, and most of the time, her face turned away, she muttered, curses I suppose.

She dragged me past Miss Jane's sweet shop. I'd often been there with my older sister before she left. Miss Jane was an old coloured lady whose small house was on the way to the Botanical Gardens and her sweets were not only delicious but very cheap. There you could get a small jar of freshly made guava jelly for a penny. The base of most of the other sweets was syrup - mixed with shredded coconut, a tablette, with ginger, a ginger cake. The most expensive were made of clarified sugar and cashew nuts. Those, I think, were threepence. The strangest was a sweet which was called lassi mango, if that is how it is spelt. When it was broken it would stretch indefinitely. The game was for one child to take one end, the other child the other, and go in different directions. At last it would be an almost invisible thread, and the joke was to watch someone walk into it and slap themselves, trying to account for the stickiness. Past all these delights Meta would drag me, taking not the faintest notice of my efforts to escape and jerking me if I looked back.

It was Meta who talked so much about zombies, soucriants, and loup-garoux (werewolves) in the West Indies. Soucriants were always women she said, who came at night and sucked your blood. During the day they looked like ordinary women but you could tell them by their red eyes. Zombies were black shapeless things. They could get through a locked door and you heard them walking up to your bed. You didn't see them, you felt their hairy hands round your throat. For a long time I never slept except right at the bottom of the bed with the sheet well over my head, listening for zombies. I suppose someone came in and pulled it down or I would have suffocated.

She also taught me to fear cockroaches hysterically. She said that when I was asleep at night they would fly in and bite my mouth and that the bite would never heal. Cockroaches can be about two inches long, they fly and they smell very disagreeable, but it was Meta who taught me to be truly afraid of them. It didn't help that my mother who tackled centipedes with great spirit, would go out of the room if a cockroach flew in and refuse to come back until it had been caught. Meta also told me that if a centipede was killed all the different bits would be alive and run into corners to become bigger, stronger centipedes. It must be crushed. She said 'mashed up'. To this day I'm not quite sure if I really saw two halves of a centipede walking away from each other, still alive.

Even Meta's stories were tinged with fear and horror. They all ended like this: 'So I went to the wedding and they say to me "What you doing here?" I say, "I come to get something to eat and drink." He give me one kick and I fly over the sea and come here to tell you this story.'

ASSIGNMENT

▶ *On your own*

Jean Rhys's piece is built around two contrasting elements: her memories of Meta's 'terror' and the pleasant recollections of Miss Jane's sweetshop. The link is Meta's refusing to let Jean visit the shop.

What is one of the worst memories of your own childhood? A constant source of anxiety, of fear, of uncertainty? Maybe it was a person or a place; a superstition or a wild story someone had told you; something you'd seen or read about which haunted your dreams . . . or just some private embarrassment.

And what was one of the pleasantest things you recall? A place you loved to visit? A favourite sweet or toy or game? Somebody who always made things right? A fantasy you would escape into when life got cruel or unfair?

Either: Write a piece of your own about something you remember warmly from your childhood.

Or: Write about something which made you edgy and unhappy.

Or: Write about a situation in which (as in Jean Rhys's piece) both good and bad things are remembered for the contrast they make.

23 Poetry workshop (v)

▶ *In small groups*

Gerda Mayer last saw her father, Arnold Stein, before the outbreak of World War Two. He was sent to the German concentration camp in Nisko in 1939. He managed to escape from there and make his way to Lemberg/Lwow, which at that time was occupied by the Russian army. He disappeared in the summer of 1940. Maybe he died in a Russian camp . . .

Make Believe

Say I were not sixty,
say you weren't near-hundred,
say you were alive.
Say my verse was read
in some distant country,
and say you were idly turning the pages:

The blood washed from your shirt,
the tears from your eyes,
the earth from your bones;
neither missing since 1940,
nor dead as reported later
by a friend of a friend . . .

Quite dapper you stand in that bookshop
and chance upon my clues.
That is why at sixty
when some publisher asks me
for biographical details,
I still carefully give
the year of my birth,
the name of my hometown:

GERDA MAYER born '27, in Karlsbad,
Czechoslovakia . . . write to me, father.

THINKING/TALKING POINTS

◆ Explain in your own words just why Gerda Mayer always gives her publishers such precise autobiographical details.

◆ What other situations can you think of in which a child might lose touch with a parent for many years?

◆ Imagine a parent and child, each living in their separate worlds, not sure whether the other is still alive.
What feelings might the child be having about that parent?
What feelings might the parent be having about the child?

◆ Imagine one of them finding out where the other was. What things might persuade him/her to make contact?

ROLE-PLAY

▶ *In pairs*

Imagine a parent and child meeting after many years apart. Discuss a few possible situations before deciding which one to improvise. Here are some suggestions:

◆ the child might have been adopted at birth

◆ the parents might have separated on bad terms – now the one who lived with the child has died

◆ the parent might have been lost in an accident and spent many years in a hospital or been taken prisoner and presumed dead

◆ the child might have run away from home

◆ the child might have been kidnapped

◆ the parents might have had a busy career which always somehow got in the way of one/either of them seeing the child – who was always at school or staying with friends . . .

Decide on the age, career, state of health, personality of your two characters.

Talk together about the mixture of feelings each of the characters might have before the reunion.

Experiment with a reunion which goes well and then with one which is just awkward, a terrible disappointment.

Maybe the parent/child just isn't what the other expected, wanted, needed, had fantasised about for so many years.

Maybe because neither expects much, they find they have everything in common . . .

ASSIGNMENT

Either: Write a letter *either* from a parent *or* from a child to the person s/he wants to believe is still there somewhere in the world. Write about what you have been doing since you were separated, what your hopes are for the future. How you feel about your long-lost parent/child.
Maybe there are some questions you would like to ask him/her. Maybe you'll post the letter just hoping that by some miracle it will find the right address . . .

Or: Write a series of diary entries covering the days before, during and immediately after a reunion between a child and the parent s/he hasn't known.

Describe your mixed feelings, hopes, fears as you prepare for the big day.

Then the day itself - the arrangements, the waiting, the moment when you actually see each other for the first time . . . First impressions. That first conversation.

Then your feelings a few hours/day/weeks later. Has it been a wonderful reunion or a bitter anti-climax?

24 Shaping a story (iii)

▶ *On your own*

This unit is designed to help you think about how to structure a short story in which the main interest is provided by some dramatic events happening over a brief period of time.

Here are the openings of two stories written by fifteen year old students. Read each of them through a couple of times. How successful do you think each of them is:

a) in grabbing the reader's attention?

b) in setting an interesting scene in which a dramatic story can develop?

Which details do you most/least like?
Suggest ways in which either of them could be improved.

The Final Minutes

For Nagako Kuni it was just another day. True, the war had meant that rice was rationed and that custom was a little short but apart from that, it was really no different.

The sunlight streamed through the wooden slats of the blind which hung in front of her and made her squint. It was nice to live in a wooden house in the summer like this but in the winter, when the wind blew hard, it was cruelly cold.

Nagako shrugged the heavy quilt off her shoulders and ran a hand through her matted black hair. Neatly, she rolled the patterned quilt up and put it in a small cupboard in the wall next to which she had been sleeping.

Like most traditional Japanese houses, there were only two rooms. She opened the door which separated them and walked through. Although it was sunny now, it had been quite a rough night and Nagako wanted to make sure nothing had been disturbed. Her little tea shop was her whole life and if that was destroyed then she would not last long. All her family had been killed during a storm when their flimsy wooden home had been destroyed by strong winds and now she had no one.

Once she was sure that everything was in order, she returned to the bedroom-come-kitchen-come-living-room and put some more charcoal in the hibachi, which was her only source of warmth . . .

The Final Minutes

Damon Cartwright ambled along the lane, and towards the imposing grey walls of the Saint Peter's finishing school.

In contrast to the school's name, it was actually the beginning of the year, and he ambled accordingly slower. As he rounded the corner, he saw a pack of chattering first years, sounding like a flock of jays. They hastily quietened as old Bertrand, the head of the first year, appeared. Bertrand was as imposing as the school buildings, and the first years smiled hopefully at him, sensing that they would do well to stay in his good books. But Bertrand had had twenty-one years of hopeful first years smiling at him, and he wasn't impressed.

Damon glanced up at the clock tower. It read twenty-two seconds to nine in the morning. Come what may, school was conducted around the clock tower. If it was an hour slow, then school started and finished an hour later than normal. It never stopped, it just ground on inexorably. Damon saw he had twenty-two seconds to get to assembly before the door was locked and even the great Paovo Nurmi, recent winner of several Olympic golds, couldn't cover four hundred yards in twenty-two seconds. Damon sprinted across the grass accompanied by the strident chords of 'Glad That I Live Am I', and failed completely to arrive in time. It was one of those days.

Luckily he was caught by Mr Allgate, who was a keen cross-country runner. Allgate knew Damon was running that evening, and so he waived justice, and Damon escaped a detention.

THINKING POINTS

Imagine you are the co-writer of one of these stories. How might it develop?

Jot down some ideas before reading further.

Here is how the first story carried on:

Final Minutes (continued . . .)

After the usual breakfast of rice and tea, Nagako went about the rest of her chores, among which was the arrangement of all her products. Although it was a teashop, Nagako sold many other things such as small, hand-made ornaments and decorative fans and with the help of these, she just about managed to make a living.

At half-past eight it was time for the shop to open. With pride, Nagako rolled up the bamboo blind which covered the front of the shop and made some final adjustments to the positions of her goods. It was a good ten minutes before anybody walked past but she had no worries, it was always like this.

At about ten o'clock, custom began to flourish and Nagako was kept very busy. Most customers were women in their traditional kimonos, older women wearing grey and brown ones while the younger ones wore bright silk and often elaborately-decorated silk ones. The occasional man did walk by but most of them were old and hunched. Some wore the traditional kimono but some wore shirts and trousers and nearly all wore caps. Many people, including Nagako, frowned upon the influence of the West, particularly American, but still this did not seem to stop the increasing number of western products on the market.

One woman in a scarlet kimono placed a small golden ornament on the counter in front of Nagako who immediately picked up her abacus and moved the beads from side to side — the Japanese number system was awkward and clumsy and Nagako found it very annoying.

* * * * * * *

The noise of the bomber's engines almost drowned the voice of the pilot out as he asked the co-pilot for their position. The co-pilot, though, after so many hours of flying, was used to the disturbance and quickly replied 'Thirty-five miles to target sir.' The bomber plunged on through the thick, white, billowing clouds which filled the sky at forty-five thousand feet. Minutes later, the coast of Japan loomed ahead. 'Down to twenty-thousand feet,' said the pilot coolly. The plane plunged through the clouds and into the clear, vivid blue of the open sky. 'Two miles to target.' said the co-pilot, checking the altimeter.

'Drop to ten thousand.' The plane again fell. 'Target coming up.' said the co-pilot with a desperate urgency. 'Prepare to release the "Little Boy".'

The seconds ticked by agonisingly. 'Now!' The bomb fell and the pilot yanked on the rudder. A huge white flash shook the plane.

At first, Nagako had thought that it was a fly. Then the noise grew to that of a bee. Then a wasp. Then a hornet. A frightened murmur went up from the large group of people waiting to be served. Then there were shouts. A large, black, evil blob moved slowly towards them across the sky.

As it got closer, people began to run in all directions, shouting and screaming. Nagako could only stare up into the everlasting blueness in horror. There was no doubt in her mind now. The blob definitely was an aeroplane. But still she stood there transfixed. It was almost overhead now. Suddenly a small black object dropped from the plane, like a wounded bird. It fell beyond her line of vision, beyond the porcupine of buildings that was the city's industrial area. Then, there was a blinding flash and searing wave of heat.

The city of Hiroshima was no more. Its memory still lingered on but its physical presence was no more. Clouds of steam and gases rose into the air to form a brooding, evil mushroom cloud. Below, a sea of rubble.

ASSIGNMENT

Either: Use one of the openings from page 78 from which to develop your own story.

Or: Write your own complete story called 'The Final Minutes'.

It's worth taking the time to plan your story carefully. You may find these notes helpful.

Stage 1 — the situation

Begin by thinking of as many situations as you can in which a few minutes could seem to last a lifetime. Or could change somebody's life dramatically, for example:

- waiting for an interview
- sending a valentine's card
- taking an examination
- a telephone rings
- somebody gets trapped

- a birth
- a death
- a competition
- the opening/closing of a prison door
- an impending disaster . . .

Add some ideas of your own to this list.

When you have thought of a situation which interests you (perhaps because it reminds you of something exciting you have been through or read about), decide roughly what will be happening:

- at the beginning of the story
- in the middle
- at the end

Beginnings take the reader quickly into the situation, and establish the mood of the piece.
The bulk of the story, the middle, sets up expectations, rushing the reader to the climax.
The best endings are often the briefest and most unexpected.

Stage 2 — the people

In a short story there will not be time to include many people if each of them is to be interesting and convincing. The best policy is to focus upon a couple of people with strongly contrasting characters. Out of the contrast may come the tension which generates the story.

Add some ideas of your own to this list:

- a girl and her grandmother
- two rivals
- a man and a woman
- a tramp and a schoolboy

When you have decided on who your main characters will be, jot down some descriptive details about them which you can draw upon as the story develops:

◆ temperament — bully, timid, generous, devious . . .?

◆ how s/he speaks, walks, behaves . . .

◆ what s/he does for a living . . .

◆ physical features . . .

◆ clothes . . .

◆ where s/he lives . . .

Stage 3 — the setting

The third element to consider at the planning stage is where your story will be set. At what time of day or night? In which season of the year? Will the weather play an important part in your story?

Picture the setting clearly in your mind's eye and then jot down as many descriptive details as you can from which to draw as you write your narrative, for example:

◆ sunrise – glare through mist

◆ grey slate roofs

◆ village on a hill

◆ cold, sharp air

◆ empty cobblestoned streets

◆ clatter of a milk cart . . .

25 ■ Poetry workshop (vi)

THINKING/TALKING POINTS

▶ *On your own or in pairs*

What sort of person do you imagine when someone talks about a surgeon?
Which of these words would you use to describe a surgeon and her/his job?

> *caring plumbing exploring healing repairing*
> *engineering loving making controlling improving*
> *hacking cold tender detached brave lonely playing*
> *magical confused controlled humane holy proud*
> *humble wise*

Add some words of your own to any you have chosen.

Do you think you would make a good surgeon? Why/Why not? As well as the medical knowledge, what special skills and human qualities do you think a surgeon needs?

Read through this poem a few times. When you have a clear idea of the main ideas, pick out the details which you think give the reader the strongest impression of this particular surgeon's personality, of his/her attitude to the operation being performed and to the patients.

The Surgeon at 2 am

The white light is artificial, and hygienic as heaven.
The microbes cannot survive it.
They are departing in their transparent garments,
   turned aside
From the scalpels and the rubber hands.
The scalded sheet is a snowfield, frozen and peaceful.
The body under it is in my hands.
As usual there is no face. A lump of Chinese white
With seven holes thumbed in. The soul is another light.
I have not seen it; it does not fly up.
Tonight is has receded like a ship's light.

It has a garden I have to do with – tubers and fruits
Oozing their jammy substances,
A mat of roots. My assistants hook them back.
Stenches and colors assail me.
This is the lung-tree.

microbes – germs

transparent – see through

scalpels – sharp surgical knives

Chinese white – white China clay

receded – moved away
tubers – thick, swollen roots

stenches – strong unpleasant smells
assail – attack

These orchids are splendid. They spot and coil like snakes.
The heart is a red-bell-bloom, in distress.
I am so small
In comparison to these organs!
I worm and hack in a purple wilderness.

The blood is a sunset. I admire it.
I am up to my elbows in it, red and squeaking.
Still it seeps up, it is not exhausted.
So magical! A hot spring
I must seal off and let fill
The intricate, blue piping under this pale marble.
How I admire the Romans –
Aqueducts, the Baths of Caracalla, the eagle nose!
The body is a Roman thing.
It has shut its mouth on the stone pill of repose.

It is a statue the orderlies are wheeling off.
I have perfected it.
I am left with an arm or a leg,
A set of teeth, or stones
To rattle in a bottle and take home,
And tissue in slices – a pathological salami.
Tonight the parts are entombed in an icebox.
Tomorrow they will swim
In vinegar like saints' relics.
Tomorrow the patient will have a clean, pink plastic limb.

Over one bed in the ward, a small blue light
Announces a new soul. The bed is blue.
Tonight, for this person, blue is a beautiful color.
The angels of morphia have borne him up.
He floats an inch from the ceiling,
Smelling the dawn drafts.
I walk among sleepers in gauze sarcophagi.
The red night lights are flat moons. They are dull with
    blood.
I am the sun, in my white coat,
Gray faces, shuttered by drugs, follow me like flowers.

Sylvia Plath

orchids – exotic flowers

aqueducts – man made channel or bridge for carrying water
Caracalla – a Roman Emperor
eagle – symbol of Romans
repose – rest
orderlies – hospital porters
pathological – for the study of diseases

morphia – sleeping drug

sarcophagi – tombs

Look closely at the poem.

How do you imagine Heaven?
What impression of the surgeon are you given by him/her thinking of Heaven as 'hygienic'?

The surgeon could have described himself/herself as wearing rubber gloves. Instead we have 'rubber hands'. How does that detail affect the way you imagine him/her?

What do you understand by the phrase 'in my hands' (line 6)?

Look again at lines 8-10.
How would you describe the surgeon's feelings about the patient's soul?

In the second stanza, the patient's body is compared first to a 'garden', then to 'a purple wilderness'. In what ways do you think a body is like/unlike these things?

What new comparisons are developed in the third stanza?
How would you describe the surgeon's changing feelings in this part of the poem?

What do you think are the most important phrases in stanza four?
Describe how they help to change the way you feel about the speaker.

'I am the sun, in my white coat'. Comment on the way the surgeon sees himself/herself here.

Do you think we are supposed to admire her/him?

Which details in the poem as a whole do you think make us admire/dislike the surgeon?

ASSIGNMENT

Write a study of Sylvia Plath's poem, 'The Surgeon at 2 am'. Pick out half a dozen details which give you a strong impression of the surgeon's personality. Talk about the way those words and phrases affected you. At the end of the poem, how do you feel about this particular surgeon? Give your reasons.

FURTHER READING

Sylvia Plath   *Gigolo*
Ted Hughes   *Hawk Roosting*

26 Media workshop (i)

▶ *In pairs*

Materials needed: pile of recent newspapers and/or magazines; scissors, plain paper, paste sticks, file paper, rulers, pens and pencils.

Advertisements (i)

Select three advertisements, for different kinds of product. Cut them out carefully and mount them.

Use the questions below to examine each of the advertisements you have chosen. Record your answers on file paper.

Work on the first advertisement together then each work on one on your own.

Stage I

Study one advertisement for a few minutes.

1   Which of these things seem to you to be the most important thing in the advertisement:

   ◆   the product itself?
   ◆   particular words?
   ◆   the people?
   ◆   the setting?
   ◆   something else?

2   When you look away from the advertisement, what image(s) remain most strongly in your mind's eye?

3   Write down some words which seem to you to describe or capture the tone/character/class/feeling of the advertisement. You may wish to select a word or two from this list:

   *excitement   sophistication   fashion   high tech   health
   manliness   friendship   love   maternal instincts   sexiness*

   Add some words of your own to any you have chosen.

4   See if you can explain how the advertisement works on your feelings. Do you think your particular response is what the advertiser hoped for? Why?

5 What seems to you to be the purpose of this advertisement?

- ◆ to give us information?
- ◆ to promote a new product?
- ◆ to keep the brand name in the public's mind?
- ◆ to reinforce the product's 'image'?
- ◆ to give a product a new 'image'?

6 How would you describe the sort of person at whom this advertisement is aimed?

- ◆ Male or female?
- ◆ Young or old?
- ◆ Married/single?
- ◆ Wealthy?
- ◆ Job/profession?
- ◆ Interests?
- ◆ Values?

7 Consider the effectiveness of the copy (the words).
How is it written and for what purpose? Is it intended to inform, amuse, flatter, provoke, soothe . . .?
Are words used simply, confusingly, poetically, bluntly . . .?

8 How would you describe the style of the picture(s)?

glossy   arty   like news photographs   amateurish . . .?

What else in the newspaper/magazine are they most like?

9 Do you find the style of the copy and the style of the pictures to be similar/different?

Stage 2

Use the data you have gathered in your answers to these questions to write an brief study of the advertisement.

What do you feel the advertiser was hoping to achieve here?
How did s/he go about it?
Do you feel s/he was successful? Why?

27 Media workshop (ii)

ASSIGNMENT

▶ *In pairs*

Materials needed: collection of newspapers and/or magazines - some recent, some a year old, some much older . . .; scissors, plain paper, paste sticks, file paper, rulers, pens and pencils.

Advertisements (ii)

The purpose of this exercise is to look at how advertising styles have changed and assess the reasons why.

Look through some magazines which span as long a period of time as possible. See if you can find some advertisements for the same (or for a very similar) product from different periods. Cut them them out carefully and mount them.

If it is difficult to find suitable advertisements, you could use the ones on pages 90–91 for this assignment.

Use the questions below to examine the set of advertisements you have chosen. Record your answers on file paper.

Stage 1

Study the advertisements for a few minutes.

1   Which of these things seem to you to be the most important thing in each advertisement:

   ◆ the product itself?   ◆ the setting?
   ◆ particular words?   ◆ something else?
   ◆ the people?

Is this something which seems to have changed with time? Was the oldest advertisement more/less wordy than the most recent? In which advertisement is the product itself most prominent?

2   When you look away from the advertisements, what image(s) remain most strongly in your mind's eye?

3   Write down some words which seem to you to describe or capture the tone/character/class/feeling of each of the advertisements. You may wish to select a word or two from this list:

   *excitement   sophistication   fashion   high tech   health
   manliness   friendship   love   maternal instincts   sexiness*

Add some words of your own to any you have chosen.

Tomorrow will be another tiring day...

HOW BOVRIL CAN HELP-
immediately and in weeks to come

THERE are times, more than ever these days, when things become a little too much for us. The noise, the pace, the strain of life get us down. We may not be ill but we're never quite well. We tire too soon and too often.

These conditions will not change. Tomorrow will be the same. What can be done? This: we can learn from our parents and our grand-parents. We can turn to the goodness of beef; to the friendly help of Bovril.

WHAT BOVRIL DOES

Bovril is a highly concentrated extract of beef. Taken as a hot drink, its action is threefold.

Immediate stimulation. When you are depressed and low, Bovril immediately stimulates. You feel strength flowing into you.

Daily protection. Every cup of Bovril puts a little more strength into you. Its power is cumulative. Against the daily wear and tear of life, Bovril should be taken daily.

Improved appetite. Bovril's pleasant, appetising flavour stimulates your sense of taste—and increases the activity of your digestive forces. Thus you enjoy your food more—and get more benefit from it.

For these good reasons Bovril has become almost an instinct in times of stress and illness. Take your cup of Bovril daily. See how well you feel. And make sure that your home is never without this tried and trusted help and standby.

No home should be without **BOVRIL**

1953

Cooks we all know

The
'YOU'LL HAVE TO TAKE POT LUCK' TYPE

Cheerfully admits she can't cook. Delights in knowing nothing about vitamins and simply doesn't care what happens to her calories. Makes up her recipes as she goes along and nobody more surprised than she when they're successful. Produces the most marvellous meals and says it's just luck. Always thought it was her own brilliant idea to add Bovril for real beef flavour ... quite astonished to find that all the best cooks do it.

In bottles—1 oz. 10d   2 oz. 1 6d   4 oz. 2 9d   8 oz. 4 10d   16 oz. 8 -

Cook with BOVRIL

1946

Hot beefy BOVRIL really does you good

WHEN THE KETTLE BOILS
IT'S TIME
FOR GOOD HOT BOVRIL

1964

91

4 See if you can explain how each advertisement works on your feelings. Do you think your particular response is what the advertiser hoped for? Why?

5 What seems to you to be the purpose of each advertisement?

◆ to give us information?

◆ to promote a new product?

◆ to keep the brand name in the public's mind?

◆ to reinforce the product's 'image'?

◆ to give a product a new 'image'?

6 How would you describe the sort of person at whom each advertisement is aimed?

◆ Male or female?   ◆ Job/profession?

◆ Young or old?   ◆ Interests?

◆ Married/single?   ◆ Values?

◆ Wealthy?

Does the target audience for this particular advertisement seem to you to have changed or stayed more or less the same?

7 Consider the effectiveness of the copy (the words). How is it written and for what purpose? Is it intended to inform, amuse, flatter, provoke, soothe . . .? Are words used simply, confusingly, poetically, bluntly . . .? How has the style of the copy changed over the years?

8 How would you describe the style of the picture(s)?

glossy   arty   like news photographs   amateurish . . .?

How has the photographic/graphic style changed over the years?
What else in the newspaper/magazine are the advertisements most like?

9 Do you find the style of the copy and the style of the pictures to be similar/different in each case?

10 What changes in people's tastes, values, expectations, attitudes do you think are reflected in the changing ways this product has been advertised over the period? At what date did Green/health issues seem to figure most strongly? And what about Technology? Has the way women are presented/appealed to changed? What about the way men and children are presented? What other changes have you noticed?

Stage 2

Use the data you have collected in answering these questions to write a brief but detailed study of what looking at the way this product has been advertised over a particular period of time tells us about changes in advertising styles and people's values.

28 Talkshop (iii)

▶ *In small groups*

Imagine you have just left a Time Machine. You have arrived in the year 1803. Can you think of a dozen gadgets which haven't yet been invented?

Which of these things do you think were around in 1803?

sun beds	printing presses
matches	telescopes
the Polaroid camera	the Walkman
zip fasteners	plastic bags
hand grenades	motor bikes
quartz wrist watches	detergents
instant coffee	musical boxes
calculators	gunpowder
scissors	fax machines
word-processors	light bulbs
ballpoint pens	sewing machines
vacuum cleaners	aspirin

Imagine you are talking to someone living nearly two hundred years ago. Once you get used to her/his language, you'll probably find you have lots in common, plenty to talk about.

But s/he might want to hear more about life in the late twentieth century. What is this 'television' contraption you keep talking about? What precisely does it do? How does it work? What is a transmitter, exactly? And an aerial? And a phono socket?

Although we think we 'know' so much more than people used to know, do we really 'know' much more than the names of the things we take for granted? How many of us could design a toaster from scratch? Or convince someone who had never seen such a thing that an aeroplane could fly?

▶ *In pairs*

Stage 1

Decide who is **A**, who is **B**.
Partner **A** chooses one of the modern inventions from the list and tries to explain how it works.
Partner **B** listens carefully to each stage of the explanation.
Ask your partner to clarify anything which you think somebody who lived two hundred years ago might not understand.

Swap roles.

Stage 2

The real test of how well we know something is to see if we can explain it clearly and simply – in language a bright twelve year old would understand.

Partner **A** is on the phone to **B**. Explain how to set up your video recorder to tape a Channel 4 programme which begins on Tuesday next at 18.30 and ends at 19.45.

Repeat the exercise, swapping roles.

FOR DISCUSSION

▶ *In pairs or small groups*

Let's try something a little less high tech. What about describing a zip and how it works?

Discuss this account of a zip fastener. Does anything need to be changed/added? Could the account be simplified and still be clear and accurate? Are there any words which you cannot understand?

How It Works

The main parts of a zip fastener are the two chains of teeth, which are attached to strips of textile material, and the slide, which opens and closes the fastener.

Each chain consists of a large number of teeth, usually of metal, which are provided with small protrusions on the top surface and with corresponding recesses on the underside (Fig. 1). The protrusion on each tooth engages accurately with the recess in the tooth above. The two chains of teeth are slightly staggered in relation to each other.

To close the fastener, the two chains must be so brought into engagement so that the teeth on the two chains can interlock in pairs. This is achieved by the slide. At its upper end the slide comprises two divergent ducts, which join each other and merge into one duct as the lower end. The slide is so designed that the two chains of teeth are brought together at exactly the correct angle to make the protrusions interlock or one tooth engage with the recess on the opposite tooth (Fig. 2).

At each end of the zip fastener are end pieces which prevent the slide from coming off. In some zips the two halves can be separated, in which case the bottom end piece is so designed that one chain of teeth can be withdrawn from the slide, while the latter is retained by the other chain.

Zip fasteners sometimes have plastic teeth (e.g. perlon), which are of a shape rather different from that of metal fastener teeth. The chains do not consist of individual teeth, but of loops formed by a spiral coil (Fig. 3). Fasteners of this kind have the advantage that, because of the resilient properties of plastic, they are not destroyed by tearing open.

ASSIGNMENT (I)

The three diagrams which should accompany this article seem to have got lost. See if you can draw one of them them so that it illustrates the features described in the account.

ASSIGNMENT (II)

▶ *On your own or in small groups*

As a distinguished visitor from the future, you have been asked by *The British Chronicle* newspaper to produce a feature for Tuesday April 1st 1803, describing a twentieth century gadget – its uses and how it works.

Choose one of the following. Think carefully about the stages in its operations and how you will explain each stage simply and clearly – in non-technical language.

a bicycle (choose a type you know well)	*a door bell*
a microwave cooker	*a camera (any type)*
a telephone	*a fire extinguisher*
a fizzy drinks maker	*a pump (any type)*
a tin opener (manual or electric)	*a hairdrier*
a stapler	*a compact disc player*
a lawnmower (any type)	*an escalator*
a car engine	*a calculator*

You may like to begin by drawing a diagram and labelling it to help you sort out your ideas. But then see if you can present the information in everyday language in a series of logical stages – similar in style to the description of the zip fastener.

When you are satisfied with your piece, read it to others and see if they can guess what gadget you are describing. They may have suggestions about how your account could be simplified or where you may need to give your readers a bit more information.

When you have discussed your draft version, make a fair copy.

29 ▮ Talkshop (iv)

▶ *In small groups*

What is your favourite board game? Take it in turns to describe to the rest of the group briefly but precisely how it's played.

Design a Game!

Materials needed: large pieces of paper/card, scissors, glue, pens, pencils, counters, dice.

ASSIGNMENT

▶ *In pairs or small groups*

What we want your team to do is to invent a board game which you think people of your age will enjoy playing. The game should tell a story.

There's an example of a game on pages 98 and 99. You might like to look at it and play it to give you some ideas of what works well.

Here are some suggestions for your game:

◆ Around the World in 80 days
◆ School Survival
◆ Jo Jones' Teenage Years
◆ Escape!
◆ From Gutter to Glitter: the Making of a Superstar
◆ Family Life Strategy Game
◆ Journey into Space/ To the Centre of the Earth

Stage I

Begin by thinking of all the board games you know. You might want to use one as a model, for example, Snakes and Ladders, Ludo, Monopoly or one of the Fantasy Adventure games . . .

You may want to combine features of several games, for example: Chance cards, dice, trading-sessions, time-limits.

Now decide on your basic idea. The examples here are based on somebody's career through school.
Will players work alone or in teams?
What will decide who is the winner?
Will there be any time-limit?
What are the basic rules?

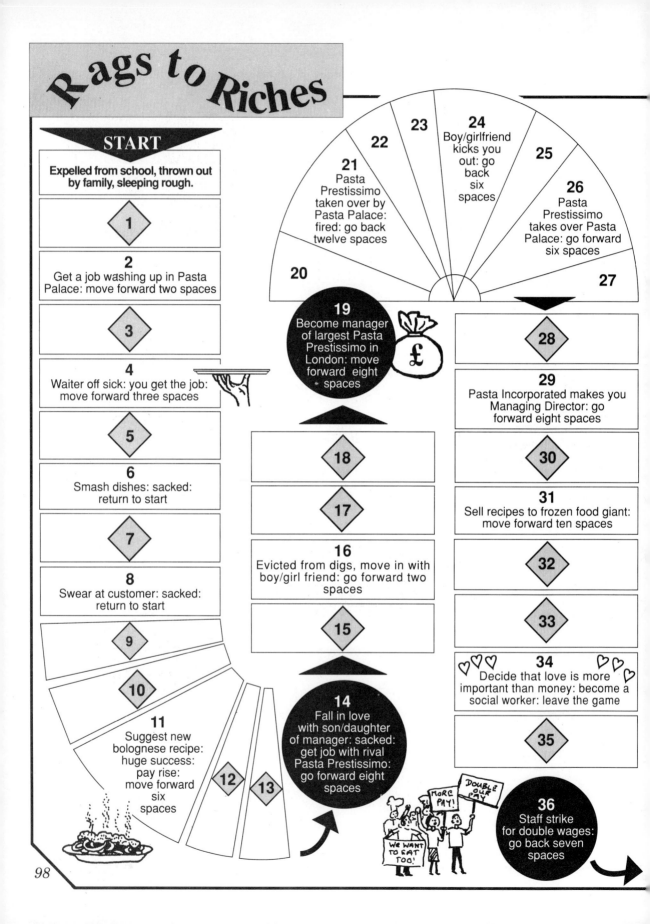

Rags to Riches

START

Expelled from school, thrown out by family, sleeping rough.

1

2 Get a job washing up in Pasta Palace: move forward two spaces

3

4 Waiter off sick: you get the job: move forward three spaces

5

6 Smash dishes: sacked: return to start

7

8 Swear at customer: sacked: return to start

9

10

11 Suggest new bolognese recipe: huge success: pay rise: move forward six spaces

12 **13**

14 Fall in love with son/daughter of manager: sacked: get job with rival Pasta Prestissimo: go forward eight spaces

15

16 Evicted from digs, move in with boy/girl friend: go forward two spaces

17

18

19 Become manager of largest Pasta Prestissimo in London: move forward eight spaces

20

21 Pasta Prestissimo taken over by Pasta Palace: fired: go back twelve spaces

22

23

24 Boy/girlfriend kicks you out: go back six spaces

25

26 Pasta Prestissimo takes over Pasta Palace: go forward six spaces

27

28

29 Pasta Incorporated makes you Managing Director: go forward eight spaces

30

31 Sell recipes to frozen food giant: move forward ten spaces

32

33

34 Decide that love is more important than money: become a social worker: leave the game

35

36 Staff strike for double wages: go back seven spaces

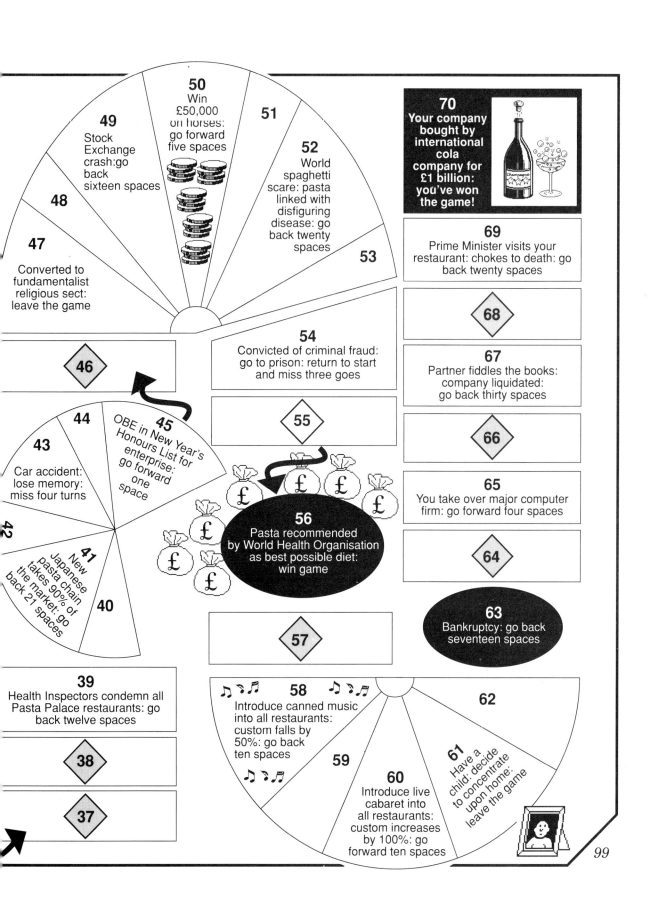

49 Stock Exchange crash: go back sixteen spaces

50 Win £50,000 on horses: go forward five spaces

51

52 World spaghetti scare: pasta linked with disfiguring disease: go back twenty spaces

53

48

47 Converted to fundamentalist religious sect: leave the game

46

54 Convicted of criminal fraud: go to prison: return to start and miss three goes

55

70 Your company bought by international cola company for £1 billion: you've won the game!

69 Prime Minister visits your restaurant: chokes to death: go back twenty spaces

68

67 Partner fiddles the books: company liquidated: go back thirty spaces

66

44

45 OBE in New Year's Honours List for enterprise: go forward one space

43 Car accident: lose memory: miss four turns

56 Pasta recommended by World Health Organisation as best possible diet: win game

65 You take over major computer firm: go forward four spaces

64

42

41 New Japanese pasta chain takes 90% of the market: go back 21 spaces

40

57

63 Bankruptcy: go back seventeen spaces

39 Health Inspectors condemn all Pasta Palace restaurants: go back twelve spaces

38

37

58 Introduce canned music into all restaurants: custom falls by 50%: go back ten spaces

59

60 Introduce live cabaret into all restaurants: custom increases by 100%: go forward ten spaces

62

61 Have a child: decide to concentrate upon home: leave the game

Stage 2

Now make a list all the good things that might happen to a player as s/he moves around the board, for example:

◆ finds himself/herself in a class with a good friend

◆ has favourite teacher for English

◆ elected form captain

◆ comes top in Maths test . . .

Now make of a list of all the worst things that could happen:

◆ only girl in a class of boys

◆ has school bully as partner in games

◆ chosen to perform in Assembly

◆ put into detention for missing bus . . .

Put some of these ideas into your game as instructions to go forward or back; up or down.

Try to introduce elements of luck and chances for recovery as well as for sudden failure:

◆ you win £100 in school lottery

◆ your bike is stolen and you lose your job

Try to make the playing of the game as full of variety as possible: there might be different kinds of activity at different stages of the game.

Stage 3

When you have made your board and all the bits and pieces, make a clear summary of the rules and then swap your game with one which another group has made. Try the games out. When you've tried out each other's games, if there's time, discuss how the games could be improved further.

Checklist

The checklist on pages 102 to 105 is designed to help teachers keep track of which units have been covered and when, particularly in supply or cover lessons.

The checklist summarises the kinds of work each unit covers so that a balanced programme of activities can be planned where a class is using the book over a longer period of time. It also suggests how long each unit is likely to take.

This is a complete version of the poem which appears on p.68.

Her Husband

Comes home dull with coal-dust deliberately
To grime the sink and foul towels and let her
Learn with scrubbing brush and scrubbing board
The stubborn character of money.

And let her learn through what kind of dust
He has earned his thirst and the right to quench it
And what sweat he has exchanged for his money
And the blood-weight of money. He'll humble her

With new light on her obligations.
The fried, woody chips, kept warm two hours in the oven,
Are only part of her answer.
Hearing the rest, he slams them to the fire back

And is away round the house-end singing
'Come back to Sorrento' in a voice
Of resounding corrugated iron.
Her back has bunched into a hump as an insult.

For they will have their rights.
Their jurors are to be assembled
From the little crumbs of soot. Their brief
Goes straight up to heaven and nothing more is heard of it.

Checklist

Unit	Skills	Number of Sessions	Completed *(Date/Initials)*
1 Making a poem (i)	◆ small group discussion ◆ group performance of a poem ◆ writing a poem using a model	1/2	-------------
2 Talkshop (i)	◆ talking and listening ◆ developing a narrative from a picture strip ◆ narrative from different points of view	1	-------------
3 Narrative writing (i)	◆ reading and discussing a poem ◆ understanding ambiguity ◆ writing a narrative using the poem as a model	2	-------------
4 Poetry workshop (i)	◆ reading and understanding a poem ◆ writing a narrative from an alternative point of view ◆ writing an original narrative	1	-------------
5 Descriptive writing (i)	◆ creative writing workshop	2	-------------
6 Making a poem (ii)	◆ brainstorming ◆ using a thesaurus ◆ refining vocabulary ◆ shaping a poem	2	-------------
7 Short story workshop (i)	◆ close study of a ghost story ◆ writing a critical essay ◆ narrative writing using the story as a stimulus	3	-------------
8 Working from pictures (i)	◆ image analysis ◆ translating a photograph into a picture in words ◆ imaginative writing in response to a photograph	1	-------------

Checklist

Unit	Skills	Number of Sessions	Completed (Date/Initials)
9 Working from pictures (ii)	◆ discussing a photograph ◆ imaginative writing in response to the photograph	1	------------
10 Poetry workshop (ii)	◆ group discussion ◆ listening and talking (pairwork) ◆ reading and discussing a poem ◆ autobiographical writing ◆ role-play	1/2	------------
11 Descriptive writing (ii)	◆ reading followed by discussion ◆ looking at pictures and recalling them ◆ writing descriptions from photographs	1	------------
12 Poetry workshop (iii)	◆ group discussion ◆ reading and discussing a poem ◆ role-play ◆ imaginative writing arising from a poem	1	------------
13 Narrative writing (ii)	◆ reading a poem ◆ drawing a picture suggested by the poem ◆ writing a continuation ◆ imaginative writing	3	------------
14 Talkshop (ii)	◆ inventing a scenario using prompts ◆ improvisation ◆ performing a poem ◆ discussing the poem ◆ writing a playscript	2/3	------------

Checklist

Unit	Skills	Number of Sessions	Completed (Date/Initials)
15 Shaping a story (i)	◆ reading and discussing a narrative extract ◆ prediction ◆ writing a continuation	1	-------------
16 Shaping a story (ii)	◆ discussing photographs ◆ brainstorming ◆ prediction exercise ◆ making a storyboard ◆ writing a narrative	2	-------------
17 Narrative writing (iii)	◆ group discussion ◆ planning a narrative	2	-------------
18 Autobiography (i)	◆ studying a short story ◆ personal writing using the story as a model	2	-------------
19 Short story workshop (ii)	◆ discussion ◆ study of a short story ◆ inventing an extra episode ◆ writing a sequel	2/3	-------------
20 Poetry workshop (iv)	◆ cloze exercise followed by discussion ◆ narrative writing prompted by the poem	1	-------------
21 Punctuation workshop	◆ exploring punctuation ◆ setting out conversation	1	-------------
22 Autobiography (ii)	◆ reading together ◆ group discussion ◆ autobiographical writing	2	-------------

Checklist

Unit	Skills	Number of Sessions	Completed *(Date/Initials)*
23 Poetry workshop (v)	◆ reading and discussing a poem ◆ role-play ◆ imaginative writing arising from the poem	1/2	----------
24 Shaping a story (iii)	◆ brainstorming ◆ shaping a narrative ◆ prediction ◆ writing a continuation ◆ writing an original story	2/3	----------
25 Poetry workshop (vi)	◆ detailed study of a poem ◆ writing a critical essay	2/3	----------
26 Media workshop (i)	◆ examining advertisements ◆ writing about advertisements	1/2	----------
27 Media workshop (ii)	◆ examining advertisements ◆ writing advertisements	1/2	----------
28 Talkshop (iii)	◆ group discussion ◆ talking and listening in pairs ◆ further groupwork: examining technical writing ◆ drawing diagrams using text ◆ technical writing – drafting/redrafting	3	----------
29 Talkshop (iv)	◆ talking and listening ◆ inventing a game using a model	3	----------

Acknowledgements

The Authors and publisher would like to thank the following for permission to reproduce from copyright material:

'Eye for an Eye' from *More Frustration* by Claire Bretecher, reprinted by permission of Methuen London. 'Ten Pence Story', reprinted by permission of Bloodaxe Books Ltd from: *Zoom* by Simon Armitage (Bloodaxe Books, 1989). 'Love Letter' by Sylvia Kantaris, reprinted by permission. 'Parents' Sayings' from *When Did You Last Wash Your Feet* by Michael Rosen, reprinted by permission of Scholastic Publications Ltd. 'Don't Interrupt' by Demetroulla Vassili, from *City Lines*, reprinted by permission of English & Media Centre. 'Power-Cut' by Joan Aiken taken from *A Book of Contemporary Nightmares* edited by Giles Gorden, published by Michael Joseph Ltd. 'Child On Top Of A Greenhouse' from *Collected Poems* by Theodore Roethke, 'Her Husband' from *Selected Poems* by Ted Hughes and 'The Surgeon At 2 a.m.' from *Collected Poems* by Sylvia Plath, reprinted by permission of Faber and Faber Ltd. 'Brer Nancy', reprinted by permission of Faustin Charles. 'Conversation Piece' from *Selected Poems of Robert Graves*, reprinted by permission of A. P. Watt Ltd on behalf of The Trustees of the Robert Graves Copyright Trust. 'Between the Lines' copyright © Carole Satyamurti 1987. Reprinted from *Broken Moon* by Carole Satyamurti (1987) by permission of Oxford University Press. 'The Threepenny Tip' by Mark Maplethorpe from the Daily Mirror Children's Literary Competition, reprinted by permission of Syndication International Ltd. 'It Must Be Different' by Morley Callaghan © The Estate of Morley Callaghan. 'Make Believe' from '*A Heartache of Grass*' by Gerda Mayer (Peterloo Poets, 1988). 'Smile Please' by Jean Rhys from an unfinished autobiography called *Smile Please*, reprinted by permission of Andre Deutsch Ltd.

Thanks are due to the following for permission to reproduce photographs:

p.29 International Museum of Photography at George Eastman House. p.31 Sally and Richard Greenhill. p.38 Mail Newspapers/Solo. p.39 (top) Express Newspapers. p.39 (bottom) Guardian Manchester Evening News. p.52 (top) Jeff Wood. p.52 (bottom) Henri Cartier-Bresson/Magnum. p.53 (top) Jeff Wood. p.53 (bottom) © Willy Ronis. pp.90-91 CPC (United Kingdom) Ltd for the Bovril advertisements.